MOTOR-CARS

D0525680

ACKNOWLEDGMENTS

The author and publishers are indebted to the following for the use of their illustrations in this book.

Alfa-Romeo, Milan, 77; Bayerische Motoren Werke AG, Munich, 101; Bond Cars Ltd., 144; Bristol Cars, 112; British Leyland (Austin-Morris) Ltd., 72, 81, 87, 89, 91, 106, 108, 110, 117, 119, 120, 135, 136, 141, 145; Buick Motor Division, Flint, Michigan, 35; Chevrolet Motor Division, 60, 98, 150; Chrysler International, 96, 142; Automobiles Citroën, Paris, 95, 129; Ferrari, Modena, 146, 153; Fiat S.P.A., Turin, 24, 34, 51, 62, 69, 92, 102; Ford Motor Co. Ltd., 75, 94, 151; General Motors Ltd., 23, 29, 44, 50, 139; Jaguar Cars Ltd., 2, 99, 116, 124, 138; Jensen Cars, 152; Lancia & Co., Turin, 122; NSU, Neckarsulm, 132; Officine Alfieri Maserati, Modena, 131; Montagu Motor Museum, 37, 40, 41, 49, 54, 63, 66, 70, 71, 74, 76, 82, 83, 84, 85, 86, 88, 100, 109, 121, 126; Automobiles Peugeot, Paris, 55, 118; Dr.-Ing. H. C. F. Porsche KG, Stuttgart, 140; Renault Ltd., 90, 113, 130; Rolls-Royce Ltd., 32, 39, 103, 115, 147; Rootes Motors Ltd., 134, 143; The Rover Co. Ltd., 33, 125, 148; Standard-Triumph Sales Ltd., 38, 111, 114; Van Doorne's Automobiel Fabric, Eindhoven, 133; Vauxhall Motors Ltd., 13, 56, 104, 127; Volkswagenwerk, Wolfsburg, 105, 137, 149; Aktiebolaget Volvo, Gothenburg, 128.

CHASSIS *Suspension (front)* Independent coil springs *(rear)* Independent coil springs *Brakes* Disk

ENGINE *Tank capacity* 23 galls. *No. of Cyls.* 6 *Carburettors* 2 S.U. *Max. B.H.P.* 245 *Capacity* 3,781 c.c.

DOORS 4

TRANSMISSION *Clutch* Single dry disk *Gearbox* 4 speed synchromesh and reverse

STEERING Power assisted rack and pinion

DIMENSIONS, ETC.
Four-five seater *Length* 15 ft 9 ins *Width* 5 ft 9 ins *Wheelbase* 9 ft 0¾ ins *Height* 4 ft 5 ins *Weight* 30½ cwt *Average speed* 115 m.p.h. (2.8 litre), 125 m.p.h. (4.2 litre)

Jaguar XJ6 Saloon 1968 'Car of the Year'

MOTOR-CARS
A picture history

Series Editor: V. C. Wall, T.D., C.Eng., M.I.Mech.E., F.R.A.S.

Compiled by Colin Munro

A PICCOLO BOOK

PAN BOOKS LTD · LONDON

First published 1970 by Ward Lock Ltd.
This edition published 1971 by Pan Books Ltd.,
33 Tothill Street, London, S.W.1

© WARD LOCK LIMITED 1970

ISBN 0 330 02877 4

Also available in this series
LOCOMOTIVES: A picture history. Compiled by Brian Reed
AIRCRAFT: A picture history. Compiled by Maurice Allward
SHIPS: A picture history. Compiled by Laurence Dunn

MADE IN ENGLAND
PRINTED IN GREAT BRITAIN
BY BUTLER & TANNER LTD
FROME, SOMERSET

From the dawn of history until the 19th century, it was only possible to travel on land at the speed of the fastest horse. Men had often wished for some better, faster means of transport, but, although Bacon prophesied in the thirteenth century that 'One day we shall endow chariots with incredible speed without the aid of any animal', no advance was made until the possibility of using the steam engine to make a self-propelled vehicle occurred to inventors.

The first mechanically-propelled passenger vehicle which actually worked was the artillery steam tractor built in France by Nicolas Cugnot, an artillery officer in the French Army. His first engine ran in the year 1769. He built a second, larger vehicle which still exists in a museum in Paris, and while this also worked, the limitations of such a vehicle—so far ahead of its time—were such that it was stored in the arsenal where it was built for many years before being moved to its present home. The top speed of this huge vehicle was about 3 miles an hour, and it had to stop to be refuelled and to get up steam about every 15 minutes. Although his tractor never towed cannon for the French Army, Cugnot seems to have been the first man to drive a mechanically-propelled vehicle.

Some thirty years later, English steam engineers were the best in the world, and in 1801 the Cornish engineer Richard Trevithick built a steam coach that was quite a success. Unfortunately it was destroyed at Christmas time when the owner celebrated a successful run in the local inn and forgot about his coach, which caught fire and burned down the shed in which it had been placed for the night. In 1803 Trevithick built a second coach which he brought to London but at that time nobody was interested in such an idea.

Once Europe had recovered from the Napoleonic wars and the steam engine had had the advantage of another twenty years of development, there was a sudden rush to build steam coaches. Many were constructed, those of Burstall and Hill, James and Anderson and Maceroni and Squire all being quite successful in their way. By far the most successful were the coaches built by Walter Hancock. He built nine in all, giving them such romantic names as 'Era', 'Enterprise' and 'Automation' and they were used for a short while to provide a bus service in London, carrying over 4000 passengers in the summer of 1834.

A few more years of such development would have seen the steam coach established as a practical means of transport, but the City of London was now investing in the railway. The City suspected that the steam coach might be a strong rival to their investment and so they, and the people who had similar vested interests in horses and the industries associated with them, had a bill passed in Parliament imposing, amongst other things, a speed limit of 4 m.p.h. A man had to proceed in front of the coach on foot carrying a red flag, and there were strict limits as to where a driver could get water for the boiler. As a result, traction engines for agricultural purposes were the only vehicles built for road use in Britain for thirty years, although the man with the red flag was abolished in 1878.

As a result of all this foolishness, the lead passed across the Channel to France and Germany. In 1860 a Frenchman, Jean Joseph Etienne Lenoir, developed an electrically ignited two-stroke internal combustion engine running on town gas. This engine was used for industrial purposes. In 1862, Lenoir attached one of his engines to a horse-drawn vehicle and made it go fairly well, although the top speed was only about walking pace. This was the first internal-combustion motor vehicle. In Germany, a Dr. Otto designed a similar engine working on the four-stroke principle (like the engines of today), and Dr. Otto is really the father of the present day car engine.

By 1872 the Otto engine was a commercial proposition. Employed at the Otto factory was one Gottlieb Daimler, who after a few years left the firm to start up on his own. His engines were successful and after a few years, together with his friend Wilhelm Maybach, he started work on a motor cycle, which also worked. After this, they tried fitting a motor to a normal carriage bought from the local coach builder. This proved to be a very clumsy affair and they decided to design a complete car.

Carl Benz had, in the meantime, been working in Karlsruhe on a motor tricycle and this was tested in 1885. It reached 8–10 m.p.h. After some development work it was put into production and offered for sale—the world's first private motor-car. In 1890 the car was redesigned with two front wheels, and in this form it remained in production until 1901.

In the meantime, things had been progressing in France. The Bollée bell foundry became enthusiastic over the steam coach and built many, of varying design. One of them, 'L'Obeissante', could carry about 10 passengers at a speed of up to 25 m.p.h. This vehicle weighed 4 tons and had independent suspension on the front wheels. Not bad for 1873!

In 1881 the Count De Dion, a rather flamboyant Parisian man-about-town, hired Georges Bouton and his brother-in-law Trépardoux to make steam vehicles for him. They were very successful, and De Dion Bouton steam cars were amongst the best you could get in the 1880s.

In the year 1888 Daimler designed a v-twin engine that developed about $3\frac{1}{2}$ h.p., which was quite powerful at that time. This was sold in France by the firm of Panhard-Levassor. It was Emile Levassor who designed the motor-car as we know it today, with the engine at the front, and with a gear-box and clutch driving the rear wheels, via a chain; his vehicles usually being fitted after the first few years with a differential. This car was very successful and it was sold in large numbers.

Enthusiasts in England watched all this with pangs of jealousy and regret that they were prevented from enjoying

Nicolas Cugnot's Steam
Tractor, 1770

these new developments by a stupid law then thirty years old. Eventually in November 1896 the old acts of 1865 and 1878 were repealed and it became legal to drive a car on the roads of England. (The first car to run on a road in England was a Panhard-Levassor, in June 1895.) For several years, all the cars in the country were imported or built under licence while British factories learned how to construct a car that would work. Some expensive mistakes were made by firms who had little engineering experience, but by the beginning of this century, the British industry had learned the hard way and were starting to build some usable motor-cars.

During the last years of the 19th century, there were no outstanding developments in motoring. Manufacturers improved their cars in a slow and steady sort of way but for several years there was little advancement.

The first motor race was held in France in June, 1895—from Paris to Bordeaux and back—a distance of 732 miles. Of 22 starters, 11 reached Bordeaux, and only 9 completed the round trip. The winner was Emile Levassor on a Panhard-Levassor.

This race was also remarkable for the first appearance of the pneumatic tyre—on a Peugeot entered by the Michelin brothers. They had many punctures and had to retire, but the car went so well when the tyres held air that the point was made that a car's performance was improved by pneumatic tyres and other makers started to fit them. For years, the Michelin tyres were the best that could be obtained, especially for racing.

In 1898, the Bollée factory in France produced some racing cars with streamlined bodies but as the engine was rated as 8 h.p., the performance was not really startling, although the average speed achieved in the 1898 Paris-Amsterdam race—26 m.p.h.—was really high speed motoring for the time.

Very soon, motor racing captured the imagination of the peoples of Europe. The result was the series of races over normal roads from Paris to Berlin, Vienna and Bordeaux, and other events ending in the famous Paris-Madrid race in 1903. This was a 'Golden Age' of motor racing, never to return. To secure the power needed to achieve the speed necessary to win, manufacturers made larger and larger engines, putting them in light, often reinforced wooden, chassis which, in many instances were not strong enough to carry the powerful engines over the rough roads of the period at the high speeds suddenly obtainable. Whereas the winner of the Paris-Amsterdam race won at an average speed of 26 m.p.h. the winner of the last city-to-city race, Gabriel, driving a 70 h.p. Mors, with a capacity of 12 litres, in the Paris-Madrid race of 1903 averaged 65.3 m.p.h. before the race was stopped at Bordeaux because of the number of accidents. This was the age when the racing car was an enormous machine, which gobbled up petrol, oil and tyres at a frightening rate. Some of these huge cars were bought by the very wealthy and fitted with touring bodies, but few lasted very long, and the running costs must have been staggering, even in those days.

In 1902, the Mercédès car was introduced by the Daimler Company in Germany. It was named 'Mercédès' after the daughter of the Company's chief agent in the south of France in the hope of marketing something that did not sound so Germanic as Daimler. The Mercédès caused quite a stir when it appeared, and it is now considered to be the first really modern motor-car.

In the U.S.A. in the first years of this century, motor builders realised almost at once that the motor-car was just what America needed to open up the vast territories between the railways. Early American cars tended to be rather more simply made than European ones, and use was made of materials that could be repaired out in the remoter parts of the country. Repairs were often made by a good blacksmith, working from the well-produced hand-books with which many makes were provided.

With the idea of providing transport for the many people who vitally needed it, series production was started in America far sooner than in Europe—where the motor-car was still something of a rich man's toy, although by 1905 many of the less conservative doctors were using a car on their rounds. By this time the motor-car had become a reliable machine, fitted with comfortable coach work. Until the First World War, it was quite normal to buy a chassis and get the body built by 'your coachbuilder' to your specification. The results on the whole were quite delightful. Few cars built today can provide the pleasure that can be had from a large touring car of this period. As you sweep effortlessly along the roads at a comfortable speed, in a pre-1914 car with its slow-revving engine, you feel that this really *is* motoring.

The appearance of the body design improved as the years went past, although some very ugly designs were produced in 1910 and 1911. In this period the high tension magneto was fitted to supply the ignition on almost all cars. It proved a great improvement on the various other systems that had been used before, such as the trembler coil, platinum tube and even the low-tension magneto which is not such a mechanically neat system. The magneto was to be used for the next 25 years or so on almost all petrol-driven vehicles, private or commercial.

Electric lights had been tried at quite an early date, but the life of a bulb was very short, partly because of vibration. It was not until about 1910 that any progress was made, and most cars were fitted with paraffin side and tail lamps and acetylene headlamps until the War.

In America the firm of Cadillac soon became one of the technical leaders of the industry, and in 1912 introduced an integrated electric light and ignition system, together with an electric starter; but it was several years before the majority of European manufacturers followed their example.

In the competition world, engines continued to get bigger up until about 1911, when it was realised that a smaller, efficiently designed engine could produce as much power, or even more power, than the monsters of previous years. Pomeroy at Vauxhall's and Henry at Peugeot were the leaders in this field, and soon all the companies engaged in motor racing were building smaller and more efficient engines, and their cars became more manageable as a result. In 1914 Mercédès made one of their periodic sallies into racing. At the French Grand Prix at Lyons, they won with a car of only $4\frac{1}{2}$ litres; yet the top speed of this car was over 110 m.p.h., showing the considerable strides that had been made in engine design. The engine of the winning car was to prove remarkably similar to the Mercédès engines being fitted to aeroplanes intended for the German Army.

By the time the First World War put a stop to motor-car production—in Europe at least—large numbers of cars were in use, both in Europe and America. The great American automobile factories in Detroit and elsewhere were turning out cars in much larger quantities than the factories of other countries, and the Ford plant at Dearborn was already well into its fantastic run of 15 million Model 'T' Fords built between 1908 and 1927. After the outbreak of war, most European car factories turned over to making shells and other munitions for the front, although, of course, the army needed a certain number of staff cars, and there was a constant demand for ambulances, lorries and buses for troop transport.

Many car factories soon found themselves making engines for aeroplanes, and by the end of the war some were building aero engines of very high performance. Unfortunately, many of the companies concerned failed to profit by this useful experience and when the war ended did not apply what they had learned to the design of their new cars.

After the war ended, thousands of men were released from the forces who, during the war, had learned to drive and look after motor vehicles, and who wanted one of their own. For a few years, there was a huge demand for cars and then the high prices caused a slump and quite a number of smaller manufacturers went out of business. Many very good cars were built in the twenties, some closely resembling the cars built before the war, others new and up-to-date.

In England, a new system of motor taxation was introduced that was to have long-lasting effects. Cars were taxed by their R.A.C.-rated horse-power, and for most of the 'twenties and 'thirties a motorist had to pay £1 per h.p.! People did not want to pay such vast sums in tax, and as a result, cars tended to become smaller. A Rolls-Royce Silver Ghost cost £45 per year in tax and in the 'twenties this was expensive. The owner of a model 'T' Ford had to pay £20 tax, for which reason it was not so popular in Britain as it was in America (and also probably the reason why not many have survived; second-hand owners just could not afford the tax). This horse-power tax, together with the tax on petrol, explains why most popular cars built in England in the period between the World Wars were of about 10 h.p. The majority of manufacturers had a car in the 9—12 h.p. range as their main seller. Examples of these—some little known today although very well known in motoring circles in the 'twenties'—are the Austin, Bean, Calcott, Calthorpe, Clyno, Gwynne, Hillman, Humber, Jowett, Morris, Palladium, Riley, Rover, Singer, Standard, Swift, Talbot, Triumph, Trojan and Wolseley cars. In addition, there was a whole host of other small 'tax cheating' cars, less well known in their day and now only remembered by the Vintage car enthusiast.

Some firms had tried four wheel brakes during the last few years before the First World War, notably Issota-Fraschini, Argyll and Arrol-Johnston, but it was not until about 1924 that four wheel brakes became at all popular. Rolls-Royce fitted them in 1924, Morris in 1925, while other firms such as Swift did not fit them until 1927.

One development of the early 'twenties was the Weymann or fabric body. The idea was to cover the wooden frame of the body with fabric (leather on an expensive car), instead of the metal panelling that was the usual system at the time. The resultant body was both lighter and quieter than the usual kind, but could get very untidy in a short space of time—although it is easier to re-cover a panel on a fabric body than to repair a damaged panel on a coach-built body.

Sports cars became very popular in the 'twenties. Cars like the 12/50 Alvis helped to establish England's reputation in this field. In France, the 24 hours race was started at Le Mans, and it was here that the name of Bentley became world famous. The exploits of the big green cars from Cricklewood, London, became a legend, and the names of the drivers, 'the Bentley Boys', were on everyone's lips. Nearly half of the Bentleys built in the 'twenties have survived, and today are very expensive collectors' pieces. Many hill climbs and rallies took place during this period and the names of the cars that won them became very well known. In Britain, Alvis, Bentley, G.N., H.E., Lagonda, Lea-Francis, Riley, Sunbeam and Vauxhall were all famous for their sports cars, while on the Continent, France's Amilcar, Bugatti, Delage, Lorraine-Dietrich and a host of cars made by smaller factories achieved constant success in rallies and races. In Italy, the names of Alfa Romeo, Fiat, Lancia and O.M. became equally well known in the sports car world.

In America—where the motor-car had become part of the normal way of life very much sooner than in Europe—the man in the street was principally interested in it as a means of getting about. In consequence, sports driving was not as popular as in Europe. Some American cars of this period, such as the Duesenberg, Packard, Cadillac and Peerless, were quite magnificent, but they were in the minority and were expensive, while the Model 'T' Ford and the Chevrolet were cheap. Already traffic was becoming a problem in the large towns, and in many states modern highways were built.

In the late 'twenties, several manufacturers tried building cars with front wheel drive, notably Tracta in France and Alvis in England, followed, a few years later, by Adler in Germany and Cord in the United States. Of these cars, only the Adler was commercially successful, although Citroen went into production with their 'traction avant' in 1934.

The great depression of 1929 had its effect on the quality of cars. Up until then, they had been built by engineers to a certain standard, but after the depression hit the pockets of the car-buying public, the salesmen took control. In many cases, engineering standards fell. Cars were fitted with smaller engines to escape the tax man, and bigger and heavier bodies to give the extra comfort that the customer demanded. The results were very often rather regrettable, although some manufacturers managed to keep going with minor changes to their old designs. The big Austin cars, for instance, continued for years with very little change.

Many manufacturers went out of business in the early thirties—and those who managed to survive did so by building cars as cheap as they could make them. Rather surprisingly, this period was a very good one for the sports car. There were races almost every weekend during the summer at Brooklands, and plenty of other events to suit enthusiasts, from Le Mans, or Monte Carlo to a rally or hill climb run by the local club. M.G. Midgets battled with Singers, Aston Martins with the famous chain-drive Frazer Nash types and the big Talbots were making their name too. On the Continent, Bugattis battled with Alfa Romeos and Maseratis, and these three makes won all the Grand Prix races. But in Germany, Adolf Hitler had come to power . . .

The German motor manufacturers were set several formidable tasks. They were to build a People's Car, produce two teams of racing cars that would win all the Grand Prix races, and provide equipment for the German Army. The people's car was designed by Ferdinand Porsche and the Nazi Party financed its development, although no cars were available for sale to the public before the start of the Second World War. During the war, two versions were built in very larger numbers—the Kubelwagen (a sort of small jeep) and the amphibious Schwimmwagen.

The racing cars built in Germany in the 'thirties, the Mercédès-Benz and Auto-Union, are among the most famous of all time. Because of the formula then in force, they were the most powerful ever built, and won most of the races they entered, although the Auto-Union was difficult to drive. The only other driver who could compete with the Germans was the almost legendary Nuvolari. At the wheel of cars with only half the power of the big German cars, he managed to win races by sheer skill and nerve. The

The Earl of Ranfurly's Vauxhall
Hansom, 1905

stories about him make fascinating reading, and many people regard him as the greatest racing driver yet.

The success of the German motor-car industry in equipping the German Army does not need retelling. Without it there could have been no Blitzkrieg, and the name of Porsche ranks high among the designers of tanks.

In France Citroen started mass production of their 'traction avant' model, the first car with chassis-less construction to be put into large-scale production. It was a very advanced design for its day and, with various modifications, remained in production for nearly twenty years.

During the 'thirties synchromesh gear-boxes became standard, an innovation pioneered by Cadillac in 1929. Hydraulic brakes were becoming more popular, but many manufacturers did not fit them until a year or two before the outbreak of war in 1939. Coil ignition had largely replaced the magneto in the early 'thirties, chiefly on the grounds of cost. A magneto tends to need rewiring every four or five years, while the coil will last very much longer, but the magneto has some advantages however, not the least being that it is quite independent of the battery. Indeed, most cars built before the First World War had no battery, unless the car was a Model 'T' or had electric lamps!

The last few years before the war saw the British car firms setting up 'shadow factories' to build aero engines and aeroplanes for the now rapidly expanding R.A.F.; also vehicles for the army which was growing and becoming more mechanised. As a result, many of the cars built in this period were good and reliable but not very exciting, the attention of the most skilled workers being directed elsewhere! Rolls-Royce had bought Bentley Motors. The Rolls-Royce-built Bentley was a magnificent car, while the Phantom III was a very complicated and advanced vehicle, rather too expensive for its day. Rolls-Royce was also very busy organising production of their 'Merlin' aero engine, without which the Battle of Britain would not have been won.

With the outbreak of war in 1939, all private car production ceased. The car factories went over to building tanks, lorries, aero engines and aeroplanes and continued doing so until 1945. Many factories in Britain and Europe suffered considerable damage during the war. Those at Coventry were very badly damaged by air raids in 1941, the Renault factory likewise was heavily hit, and most German factories were completely gutted. Much of the German factories' equipment was moved to underground sites all over the country, and large quantities were captured by the Russians, who removed any machine tools that looked in any way useful. Thus, by the end of the war the Germany industry was left without factories, with hardly any equipment and with limited staff. Few other European factories were noticeably better off. Only the Americans had their industry intact, though they too had to reorganise for peace-time production.

Once the war was over and the factories on both sides of the Atlantic had managed to settle down to peacetime conditions again, car designers had a wonderful chance to start afresh. Not all of them were as far-seeing as they might have been. For instance, some British engineers sent to Germany to evaluate the motor industry there could see no commercial future for the Volkswagen! But when the first post-war cars came out of the factories, it was seen that many features that had been tried on a few models before the war were now the accepted thing. Prewar, independent suspension was something of a novelty, but now any vehicle that was not so fitted was very out of date.

A further idea, pioneered by Citroen as we have seen, was the use of a sheet-steel stressed hull to which the various mechanical components were fitted, instead of the now old-fashioned chassis to which was bolted the body. This system of construction saves considerable weight but the effects of rust on a car of this type can be quite horrifying. It is now quite usual for a car that has years of useful life left in the mechanical parts to be sent to the breaker's yard because rust has set in and eaten away the underneath of the body-work. American car manufacturers have been slow to adopt this kind of construction, for which, no doubt, many American drivers with oldish cars are very thankful.

The late 'forties and early 'fifties were chiefly notable for amalgamations and takeovers. In England, the old-established firms of Austin and Morris got together to form the British Motor Corporation. In France, Citroen bought Panhard-Levassor, then Michelin bought them both.

In the U.S.A., there were by now only two big groups, Ford and General Motors, with Chrysler and American Motors large but not in the giant league.

In Europe in the early 'fifties the car started to acquire the shape that we know today, with the Italians taking the lead in design of body-work that they still hold. The Americans had one of their more flamboyant periods and the results were mostly rather unfortunate. Sir Hugh Casson called this the age of 'tin merangue'. The Italians, on the other hand, relied on good design with simple, crisp lines and the minimum of chromium ornamentation.

Oddly enough, the Russians, who could have followed either of these styles of body design, chose to copy the more ornate American designs, so that the average Russian car tends to look rather like a smaller version of an American car of about four or five years previous. One would think that the simple lines of the best Italian designs would appeal to the Russians, but the fact is that many Russian designs are rather large and also rather ornate with lots of chromium decoration.

For the first few years after the War, there was little time or money to build new cars for motor sport, and for the first few seasons most of the competition cars were pre-war ones. A new formula came into force on the first of January, 1947, for Grand Prix cars, and this induced Ferrari to re-enter the racing world, while in England the B.R.M. project was started. The original B.R.M. design was too complex.

However, when the cars did run, they were very spectacular and their performance was of a high standard. Unfortunately, they did not always finish and it was Alfa Romeo and Maserati who led the field.

In the sports car field, Jaguar C and D Types were almost unbeatable, winning for many years at Le Mans and most of the other big sports car events, both in Europe and the U.S.A. The Americans had become much more interested in better sports car since the war, and by the early 'fifties were organising sports car events with enthusiasm. Other sports cars built in England about this time were the Allard, using large American engines in British chassis, the Austin-Healey, and later the famous Triumph TR series of sports cars, using Standard Vanguard engines. These all proved to be best sellers.

In the 'fifties, too, there were various experiments using gas turbines for motors instead of the piston engine that we have had for so long. The best publicised of these were the cars built by Rover, who even entered into some competition with one or two of their cars. Much useful data was obtained, but we are still a long way from having production gas-turbine cars on sale to the public. In the U.S.A., work on gas-turbine commercial vehicles is so far advanced that long-range heavy vehicles are already in production in small numbers.

In Germany, N.S.U. became interested in the Wankel rotary piston engine and after some experimental work have put it into production. This is the first really revolutionary invention since the original Panhard-Levassor of 1891.

The world's motor industries are now trying to build cars that are both safer to drive and safer in the event of an accident. It would be nice to think that these cars of the future will be better lasting, but this seems unlikely. Many a 15-year-old car is literally rusting away. Purchasers of second-hand cars know where to look on any one model for signs that rust is eating away the all-too-thin metal. The design of the modern car relies on bending the thin sheet metal into complicated shapes, instead of the old-fashioned method of providing solid metal.

The ultimate in the family car is likely to be a combination of glass-fibre body with some form of electric power. The disadvantage of the electric car is exactly the same at the present time as it was in 1893 when the Jeantaud went into production—the limited performance that can be obtained from a set of batteries, and the weight of the batteries. Much money has been spent and will continue to be spent on this problem. No doubt, a solution will eventually be found.

This Steam Wagonette is one of the very early steam vehicles built in Britain. Although there was a spate of building steam coaches and similar vehicles in the 1830s, the public was prejudiced against them. In 1865, Parliament legislated against self-propelled road vehicles, and this legislation was only repealed in 1896. Little is known of the Catley and Ayes. The dimensions given are approximate.

CATLEY AND AYES STEAM WAGONETTE 1868

CHASSIS *Suspension (front)* 4 small coil springs *(rear)* $\frac{1}{2}$ elliptic *Brakes* Rear wheels only
DOORS 2
STEERING Tiller
DIMENSIONS, ETC.
Four seater *Length* 9 ft *Width* 6 ft *Wheelbase* 7 ft 6 ins *Height* 6 ft 6 ins

ROGER BENZ
1888

This Roger-Benz is a French version of the original Benz car as made from 1885–1891. The first motor-car that really ran at all well, it was fairly simple and reliable to operate and became very popular. In 1891 it was redesigned as a 4-wheel car and production continued until 1901, by which time this type was becoming almost comic. Nevertheless it was the world's first practical production motor-car.

CHASSIS *Suspension (front)* Transverse full elliptic *(rear)* Full elliptic *Brakes* Wood blocks on iron tyres, rear wheels only

ENGINE *No. of Cyls.* 1 *Carburettors* A bubble vaporizer *Max. B.H.P.* 3 *Capacity* 1,690 c.c. *Ignition* Battery and coil

TRANSMISSION *Clutch* Leather belts *Gearbox* 2 *Final Drive* Chain

STEERING Hand lever

DIMENSIONS, ETC.
Two seater *Length* 8 ft 11 ins *Width* 5 ft $1\frac{1}{2}$ in *Wheelbase* 5 ft $1\frac{1}{2}$ ins *Tyre size* 4 ft 1 × $1\frac{1}{2}$ Front wheel 30 ins × $1\frac{1}{2}$ *Height* 5 ft 8 ins without hood, 7 ft 8 ins hood up *Average speed* Max. speed 15 m.p.h.

Engine No. 394. This car is typical of the early Panhard Levassor fitted with the two cylinder Daimler engine. A similar car, fitted with a two-seater body, won the world's first car race—Paris Bordeaux Paris—in 1895 at an average speed of 15 m.p.h. This type, more or less modified, was in production from 1891 to about 1897.

PANHARD LEVASSOR PHAETON 1894

CHASSIS *Suspension (front)* Full elliptic *(rear)* ½ elliptic *Brakes* Spoon on rear tyres, external contracting on countershaft
ENGINE *No. of Cyls.* 2 *Carburettors* 1 Maybach *Max. B.H.P.* 4 *Ignition* Hot tube
TRANSMISSION *Clutch* Water cone *Gearbox* Open 3 speed and reverse. *Final Drive* Side chain
STEERING Tiller
DIMENSIONS, ETC.
Four seater *Length* 9 ft 3 ins *Width* 5 ft 4 ins *Wheelbase* 5 ft 5 ins *Tyre size* Front 32 × 1½. Rear 42 × 1½ *Height* 5 ft 9 ins *Weight* 15 cwt

LANCHESTER SECOND EXPERIMENTAL CAR 1897

The early Lanchester cars were designed and built to a very high standard indeed. The engine was much more refined than any other of the time, the gearbox had a preselector mechanism and the springing was very comfortable. Highly individual in design, Lanchesters achieved a firm following. Nowadays, almost any Lanchester is to be cared for and cherished.

CHASSIS *Suspension (front)* $\frac{1}{2}$ elliptic cantilever *(rear)* $\frac{1}{4}$ elliptic *Brakes* Rear wheels only

ENGINE *No. of Cyls.* 2 (flat-twin) *Carburettors* 1 Wick type *Max. B.H.P.* 10 h.p. *Ignition* L.T. magneto

TRANSMISSION *Clutch* Cone clutch *Gearbox* 2 speed and reverse epicyclic *Final Drive* Shaft to worm gearing

STEERING Tiller

DIMENSIONS, ETC.

Two seater *Length* 8 ft 6 ins *Width* 4 ft 5 ins *Wheelbase* 5 ft 9 ins *Tyre size* Front 30 × 2. Rear 36 × 2 *Height* 5 ft 6 ins *Weight* 14 cwt. *Average speed* 26 m.p.h.

DAIMLER CAR 1897

Cannstatt-Daimler cab, probably imported by Harry Lawson, the originator of the Motor Car Club, The Daimler Company in England and the Motor Manufacturing Company. Closed bodywork was unusual so early on, if only because of its weight. Note the wooden mudguards, the leather let-down roof and the leather cover over the driver's lap. Wheel steering was very modern in 1897.

CHASSIS *Suspension (front)* Transverse elliptic *(rear)* Elliptic *Brakes* On rear wheels only
ENGINE *No. of Cyls.* 2 *Carburettors* 1 *Max. B.H.P.* 10 *Capacity* 1,551 c.c. *Ignition* Platinum tube
DOORS 2
TRANSMISSION *Gearbox* 4 speed and reverse. *Final Drive* Chain
DIMENSIONS, ETC.
Four seater *Length* 10 ft 6 ins *Width* 5 ft *Wheelbase* 5 ft 10 ins *Tyre size* Front 32 × 1½. Rear 42 *Height* 8 ft 6 ins *Average speed* 20 m.p.h. approx.

M.M.C. TONNEAU 1897

Car No. 308. This car was built by Harry Lawson's Motor Manufacturing Company, most of whose cars were based on the Daimler designs of the period. Despite several reorganizations, sales dropped steadily and after 1908 the company no longer built cars. None of the cars was exciting.

CHASSIS *Suspension (front)* $\frac{1}{2}$ elliptic *(rear)* Full elliptic *Brakes* 'Spoon' on rear tyre and extension operating on rear wheels only

ENGINE *No. of Cyls.* 2 *Carburettors* 1 Maybach *Capacity* 1,650 c.c. *Ignition* Hot Tube

TRANSMISSION *Clutch* Leather cone *Gearbox* 3 speed and reverse *Final Drive* Chain

DIMENSIONS, ETC.
Four seater *Length* 9 ft 3 ins *Width* 5 ft *Wheelbase* 5 ft 8 ins *Tyre size* Front 31 × 1$\frac{1}{2}$. Rear 43 × 1$\frac{1}{2}$ *Height* 5 ft 9 ins

The Oldsmobile was the first car to be built in large numbers in the U.S., and being simple, reliable and not expensive, was an immediate success. It was one of the first American cars to be exported to Britain where it also became popular.
It even had a song written about it—'My Merry Old Oldsmobile'.

OLDSMOBILE CURVED DASH RUNABOUT 1900

CHASSIS *Suspension (front)* $\frac{1}{4}$ elliptic *(rear)* $\frac{1}{4}$ elliptic *Brakes* On transmission and handbrake on drums on rear wheels
ENGINE *Tank capacity* 5 galls. *No. of Cyls.* 1 *Carburettors* 1 Oldsmobile *Max. B.H.P.* 7 *Capacity* 1,840 c.c. *Ignition* Trembler coil
TRANSMISSION *Clutch* One for each gear *Gearbox* 2 speed epicyclic and reverse *Final Drive* Chain
DIMENSIONS, ETC
Two seater *Length* 8 ft 1 ins *Width* 4 ft *Wheelbase* 5 ft 6 ins *Tyre size* 30 × 3$\frac{1}{2}$ *Height* 4 ft 11 ins *Average speed* 18–24 m.p.h.

FIAT
REAR ENTRANCE
TONNEAU
12 h.p.
1901

The first Fiat appeared at the end of 1899. It had a 679 c.c. flat twin rear engine, cone clutch and chain drive. In 1901, a front-engined 1.2 litre vertical twin with central chain drive was in manufacture. The two famous racing drivers, Vincenzo Lancia and Felice Nazzaro, were among the first Fiat employees. This car is a fairly typical largish car of the period.

CHASSIS *Suspension (front)* $\frac{1}{2}$ elliptic *(rear)* $\frac{1}{2}$ elliptic *Brakes* Rear wheels only
ENGINE *Carburettors* 1 *Capacity* 3,770 c.c. *No. of Cyls.* 4 *Max. B.H.P.* 14 *Ignition* L.T. Magneto
BODY *Doors* 1
TRANSMISSION *Clutch* Leather cone *Gearbox* 3 speed and reverse *Final Drive* Side chain
DIMENSIONS, ETC. Four seater *Length* 10 ft 8$\frac{1}{2}$ ins *Width* 4 ft 9 ins *Wheelbase* 7 ft *Tyre size* 660 × 65 Front. 700 × 65 Rear *Height* 5 ft 5 ins *Weight* 21 cwt *Average speed* 55 m.p.h. approx.

Wheel steering and pneumatic tyres were introduced on most Panhards in 1898. Models of 1900 and 1901 had cylindrical controls on the steering wheel, quadrant change, automatic inlet valves, and final drive by side chains. The 1.7 litre 7 h.p. twin of 1901 sold for £340.

CHASSIS *Suspension (front)* $\frac{1}{2}$ elliptic spring *(rear)* $\frac{1}{2}$ elliptic spring *Brakes* Rear wheels only

ENGINE *No. of Cyls.* 4 *Carburettors* 1 *Max. B.H.P.* 40 approx. *Capacity* 7,433 c.c. *Ignition* Trembler coil

TRANSMISSION *Clutch* Leather cone *Final Drive* Chain

DIMENSIONS, ETC.
Two seater *Length* 11 ft 8 ins *Width* 4 ft 8 ins *Wheelbase* 8 ft 8 in *Tyre size* 870 × 80 *Weight* 1,200 kg *Average speed* 65 m.p.h. approx.

MERCEDES REAR ENTRANCE TONNEAU
35 h.p.
1902

The first Mercedes of 1901—the 35 b.h.p. 5.9 litre model—is regarded as the first modern motor-car. It had mechanically operated inlet valves, a jet carburettor, 4 cylinder engine, pressed steel frame, honeycomb radiator, and gate gearchange. Designer of the Mercedes was Wilhelm Maybach (1846–1929). It was built at Bad Cannstatt by the Daimler Motoren-Gesellschaft. In 1902 the Daimler Company adopted the name 'Mercedes' for its private cars. From the beginning, Mercedes cars won many racing competitions.

CHASSIS *Suspension (front)* $\frac{1}{2}$ elliptic *(rear)* $\frac{1}{2}$ elliptic *Brakes* Rear wheels only
ENGINE *Carburettors* 1 *Capacity* 5.9 litre *Max. B.H.P.* 35 *Ignition* L.T. Magneto
TRANSMISSION *Clutch* Mercedes 'Scroll' clutch *Gearbox* 4 speed and reverse *Final Drive* Side chain
DIMENSIONS, ETC.
Four seater *Length* 11 ft 3 ins *Wheelbase* 7 ft 10 ins *Tyre size* 910 × 90 Front. 920 × 120 Rear *Height* 5 ft *Average speed* 45/50 m.p.h.

The first four-wheel cars built by Wolseley were designed by Herbert Austin. The first cars were fitted with a single horizontal cylinder and were called a '3 h.p. car' but the production car was usually the 2 cylinder 10 h.p. model. The engine was a flat twin under the floor level. The design was quite successful, and a racing version was built and raced by such drivers as Charles Jarrot and C. S. Rolls with some success, although they were not up to the Continental racing standard.

WOLSELEY REAR ENTRANCE TONNEAU 1902-3

CHASSIS *Suspension (front)* $\frac{1}{2}$ elliptic *(rear)* $\frac{1}{2}$ elliptic *Brakes* Rear wheels only
ENGINE *Carburettors* 1 *Capacity* 2,605 c.c. *No. of Cyls.* 2 *Max. B.H.P.* 10 *Ignition* Trembler coil
DOORS 2 front, 1 at the rear
TRANSMISSION *Clutch* Leather cone *Gearbox* 4 speed and reverse *Final Drive* Chain
DIMENSIONS, ETC. *Length* 11 ft 11 ins *Width* 5 ft 11 ins *Wheelbase* 7 ft *Tyre size* 30 × 3$\frac{1}{2}$ Front. Solid rear *Height* 5 ft, with no hood *Weight* 19 cwt *Average speed* 35 m.p.h.

MORS 70 h.p.
RACING
1903

The Mors was Panhard's chief rival in early races. This car, driven by Gabriel, won the Paris–Madrid race of 1903, stopped at Bordeaux because of the high number of accidents. There was no control of spectators, who did not realize the speed of the cars. This was the last City to City race, and the end of an era. Gabriel's historic drive, in which he averaged 65 m.p.h., overtaking more than a hundred other cars during the 342 mile race represented the high point of the heroic age of motor racing!

CHASSIS *Suspension (front)* $\frac{1}{2}$ elliptic *(rear)* $\frac{1}{2}$ elliptic *Brakes* Rear wheels only
ENGINE *No. of Cyls.* 4 *Carburettors* 1 *Capacity* 11,600 c.c. *Ignition* L.T. Magneto
TRANSMISSION *Final Drive* Chains
DIMENSIONS, ETC.
Two seater *Average speed* 90 m.p.h. max.

The single cylinder Cadillac was produced from 1903 until 1908 and was a small car with a big engine which would last a long time in rough conditions. Various versions were built, types B, C, E, F, K, M, S and T, with a variety of body styles including a light van. Over 15,000 were made and so well were they built that many still exist in America.

CADILLAC "A" REAR ENTRANCE TONNEAU 1903

CHASSIS *Suspension (front)* $\frac{1}{2}$ elliptic *(rear)* $\frac{1}{2}$ elliptic *Brakes* Rear wheels only
ENGINE *No. of Cyls.* 1 *Carburettors* 1 *Ignition* Trembler coil
DOORS 1
TRANSMISSION *Clutch* 1 band per gear speed *Gearbox* 2 speed epicyclic with reverse *Final Drive* Chain
DIMENSIONS, ETC.
Four seater *Length* 9 ft 2 ins *Width* 5 ft 8 ins *Wheelbase* 6 ft 4 ins *Tyre size* 30 × 3$\frac{1}{2}$ *Height* 5 ft 6 ins (Hood down if fitted) *Weight* 10 .cwt *Average speed* 25 m.p.h. approx. max.

DE DION BOUTON REAR ENTRANCE TONNEAU 1903

De Dion Bouton was the first company to put a car into mass production. Their cars were popular, and had a good performance for their time. They were produced in surprisingly large numbers. In 1901 they were reputedly being built at the rate of 200 per month. Even today there are many De Dion Boutons in working order.

CHASSIS *Suspension (front)* $\frac{1}{2}$ elliptic *(rear)* $\frac{3}{4}$ elliptic *Brakes* Foot brake on drum behind gearbox. Hand brake rear wheels only
ENGINE *No. of Cyls.* 1 *Carburettors* 1 De Dion Bouton *Max B.H.P.* 8 h.p. *Capacity* 942 c.c. *Ignition* Trembler coil
TRANSMISSION *Clutch/Gearbox* 3 speed expanding clutch gearbox with reverse *Final Drive* De Dion axle
DIMENSIONS, ETC.
Four seater *Length* 9 ft 7 ins *Wheelbase* 6 ft 1 ins *Tyre size* 710 × 90 *Height* 4 ft 11 ins

The Darracq was one of the better known early French cars, and was exported to Britain in fair numbers. Our photo shows 'Genevieve', the car starring in the film of that name, just as it appeared in the film. A rather typical two seater of the period, 'Genevieve' is now in New Zealand.

CHASSIS *Suspension (front)* ½ elliptic *(rear)* ½ elliptic *Brakes* Foot transmission. Hand brake rear wheels only
ENGINE *No. of Cyls.* 2 *Carburettors* 1 *Max. B.H.P.* 12 *Capacity* 2,284 c.c. *Ignition* Trembler coil
TRANSMISSION *Clutch* Leather cone *Gearbox* 3 speed and reverse *Final Drive* Shaft to bevel gear
DIMENSIONS, ETC.
Two seater *Length* 9 ft 6 ins *Width* 4 ft 8 ins *Wheelbase* 7 ft 5 ins *Tyre size* 810 × 90 *Weight* 15 cwt *Average speed* 35/40 m.p.h.

ROLLS ROYCE
10 h.p.
1904

Henry Royce (1863–1933) formed Rolls-Royce in 1904 in partnership with the Hon. C. S. Rolls, a racing driver and pioneer airman. The high standard set at the beginning by Rolls-Royce has been maintained ever since.

CHASSIS *Suspension (front/rear)* Semi-elliptic springs *Brakes* Foot brake acting on drum on transmission. Hand brake, internal expanding on rear wheels

ENGINE *Tank capacity* 6 galls. *Carburettors* 1 *Capacity* 1,800 c.c. *No. of Cyls.* 2

TRANSMISSION *Clutch* Internal cone type *Gearbox* 3 forward 1 reverse, direct drive on 3rd *Final Drive* Fully floating line axle, bevel drive

DIMENSIONS, ETC.

Two and Four seater *Length* 12 ft 10 ins approx. *Width* 5 ft 8 ins approx. *Wheelbase* 75 ins *Tyre size* 810 × 90 *Height* 5 ft 8 ins approx. *Weight* 11 cwt *Average speed* 35 m.p.h.

This car sold at £200, and was the first of a long line of small cars by the Rover company. These cars had a very good reputation and were popular amongst doctors. Most subsequent Rovers had more attractive bodywork.

CHASSIS *Suspension (front)* Transverse leaf *(rear)* $\frac{1}{2}$ elliptic *Brakes* Right pedal acting on back wheel drums, left pedal acting on engine
ENGINE *No. of Cyls.* 1 *Carburettors* 1 *Max. B.H.P.* 8
TRANSMISSION *Clutch* Metal to metal single plate *Gearbox* 3 speeds forward, 1 reverse *Final Drive* Shaft to bevel gear
DIMENSIONS, ETC. Open Two seater *Length* 9 ft 6 ins *Width* 4 ft 8 ins *Wheelbase* 6 ft 6 ins *Tyre size* 750 × 65 *Weight* 9 cwt *Average speed* 24 m.p.h.

FIAT "BREVETTI" LANDAULETTE 1905

This product of the Fiat factory is a good example of the European 'town car'. The extra mudguards by the driver's seat are to prevent the bodywork and the passenger's door being splashed with mud. Note the little instruction speaker by the driver's ear, for transmitting orders from the rear compartment.

CHASSIS *Suspension (front)* $\frac{1}{2}$ elliptic *(rear)* $\frac{1}{2}$ elliptic *Brakes* Rear wheels only
ENGINE *No. of Cyls.* 4 *Carburettors* 1 *Max. B.H.P.* 20 *Capacity* 3,052 c.c. *Ignition* L.T. Magneto
DOORS 2
TRANSMISSION *Clutch* Plate *Gearbox* 4 speed and reverse *Final Drive* Shaft to bevel gear
DIMENSIONS, ETC.
Four and Two seater *Length* 14 ft 8 ins approx. *Wheelbase* 9 ft 10 ins *Tyre size* 880 × 120 Rear, 870 × 90 *Weight* 1,600 kg *Average speed* 45–50 m.p.h.

This Buick was one of the first cars built in numbers by the company, which started in 1903, and cars to this basic design were continued until 1910. It was unusual in that the 2 cylinder engine was under the front seat, and drove through a chain to the rear axle. The Buick type 'C' was not expensive and sold well.

**BUICK
SIDE ENTRANCE
TONNEAU 1905**

CHASSIS *Suspension (front)* $\frac{3}{4}$ elliptic *(rear)* $\frac{1}{2}$ elliptic *Brakes* External contracting on differential

ENGINE *No. of Cyls.* 2 *Carburettors* 1 Schebler *Max. B.H.P.* 22 *Ignition* Trembler coil

DOORS 2

TRANSMISSION *Clutch* cone *Gearbox* 2 speeds and reverse *Final Drive* Chain to rear axle

DIMENSIONS, ETC.
Four seater *Length* 11 ft 10 ins *Wheelbase* 7 ft 2 ins *Tyre size* 30 × 3$\frac{1}{2}$ *Height* 6 ft 10 ins hood up *Average speed* 35 m.p.h. approx. max.

RENAULT GRAND PRIX RACING 1906

The Renault racing cars were fairly typical cars of their period, except that the radiator and bonnet were the usual Renault design instead of the more usual arrangement with the radiator at the front. The Renault design probably gave a more even distribution of weight. These cars were quite successful in competitions.

CHASSIS *Suspension (front)* $\frac{1}{2}$ elliptic *(rear)* $\frac{1}{2}$ elliptic *Brakes* Rear wheels only
ENGINE *No. of Cyls.* 4 *Carburettors* 1 Renault *Max. B.H.P.* 105 *Capacity* 12,975 c.c. *Ignition* H.T. magneto
TRANSMISSION *Clutch* Cone *Gearbox* 3 speeds and reverse *Final Drive* Shaft to bevel gear
DIMENSIONS, ETC.
Two seater *Length* 15 ft 3 ins *Width* 5 ft 3 ins *Wheelbase* 9 ft 6$\frac{1}{4}$ ins *Tyre size* 870 × 90 Front. 880 × 120 Rear *Height* 4 ft 9 ins *Weight* 27$\frac{1}{2}$ cwt (ready to race) *Average speed* 100 m.p.h. max.

This Daimler is a typical expensive car of the middle of the first decade of this century. Note the acetylene headlamps of fairly early type, and the roof and back of the body that lets down in good weather. The dimensions varied according to the body—and mudguards—fitted.

DAIMLER 30/40 LANDAULETTE 1906

ENGINE *Tank capacity* 20 galls. *No. of Cyls.* 4 *Carburettors* 1 *Max. B.H.P.* 38 *Capacity* 7,247 c.c. *Ignition* H.T. magneto and trembler coil

DOORS 2

TRANSMISSION *Clutch* Leather cone *Gearbox* 4 speeds and reverse *Final Drive* Side chains to rear wheels

DIMENSIONS, ETC.
Four seater *Length* 14 ft 6 ins approx. *Width* 5 ft 6 ins approx. *Wheelbase* 9 ft $10\frac{1}{8}$ ins *Tyre size* Front 875 × 105. Rear 880 × 125 *Height* 8 ft 4 ins *Weight* 26 cwt chassis only *Average speed* 50 m.p.h. approx. max.

STANDARD
16–20 h.p.
1906

The Standard 16–12 is a typical touring car of about 1905/6 with a fussy design of body. Note the early use of a luggage grid at the rear and the leather apron between the chassis and the running board to keep dust away from the body. Soon after this, Standard adopted their radiator badge and shape that was to last until about 1932.

CHASSIS *Suspension (front)* $\frac{1}{2}$ elliptic *(rear)* $\frac{1}{2}$ elliptic *Brakes* Rear wheels only
ENGINE *No. of Cyls.* 4 *Carburettors* 1 *Max. B.H.P.* 25 (rated) *Capacity* 3,700 c.c.
DOORS 2
TRANSMISSION *Gearbox* 4 speeds and reverse *Final Drive* Shaft to bevel gear
DIMENSIONS, ETC.
Four seater
Length 12 ft 6 ins approx. (hood down) *Wheelbase* 8 ft 9 ins *Tyre size* 820 × 120 *Height* 5 ft 10 ins (hood down) *Average speed* 45–50 m.p.h. approx. max.

ROLLS ROYCE "SILVER GHOST" 1906

This famous model remained in production until 1926, and set standards which founded the reputation of Rolls-Royce. Its quiet, smooth-running must have been very welcome to motorists after the bone-jarring caused by previous cars. Both open and closed bodies of various designs were fitted, to suit the requirements of the customer. 'The Silver Ghost' became the standard by which to judge other cars and it is still, to this day, a very fine car to travel in.

CHASSIS *Suspension (front)* Semi-elliptic *(rear)* Platform rear spring suspension *Brakes* Footbrake, external contracting type on prop-shaft. Handbrake, internal in brake drums **ENGINE** *Tank capacity* 13 galls. *Carburettors* 1 *Capacity* 7,036 c.c. *No. of Cyls.* 6, side valve *Max. B.H.P.* 48 (rated) *Ignition* Trembler coil and magneto

TRANSMISSION *Clutch* Cone type *Gearbox* 4 speed and reverse top o'drive *Final Drive* Spiral bevel

DIMENSIONS, ETC. *Length* 180 ins *Width* 72 ins *Wheelbase* 135 ins *Tyre size* 895 × 150 *Height* Various *Weight* Chassis only 18½ cwt *Top speed* 60 m.p.h.

INTERNATIONAL HARVESTER "AUTO-BUGGY" 1907

The high wheeler was a purely American development, originating at a 1906 Motor Show. The cars were intended to supply cheap transportation for the mid-Western farmer who had long distances to travel over roads of dust. About 70 makes were produced between 1906 and 1913, by which time the Ford 'T' had taken over the market. Our picture shows an I.H.C. of 1912, restored in America.

CHASSIS *Suspension (front)* Full elliptic *(rear)* Full elliptic *Brakes* Rear wheels only
ENGINE *No. of Cyls.* 2 *Carburettors* 1 *Max. B.H.P.* 18–20 *Ignition* Magneto
TRANSMISSION *Clutch* Leather cone *Gearbox* 2 speed and reverse *Final Drive* Chains
DIMENSIONS, ETC.
Two–Six seater
Length 10 ft approx. according to type *Wheelbase* 7 ft–7 ft 8 ins *Tyre size* 40 × 1⅝ ins Front. 44 × 1⅝ Rear *Weight* 14 cwt *Average speed* 25 m.p.h. approx. max.

An Itala (not the one illustrated here) was entered by Prince Borghese in the 1907 Peking–Paris race, which it won. It had specially large tanks fitted with the third seat in the centre of the tanks and equipment carried. One of the wooden wheels was broken in Siberia and had to be rebuilt by a Russian peasant.

CHASSIS *Suspension (front)* ½ elliptic *(rear)* ½ elliptic *Brakes* Foot brake on transmission. Handbrake on drums on rear wheels

ENGINE *Tank capacity* Petrol 60 galls. Oil 20 galls. Water 10 galls. *No. of Cyls.* 4 *Carburettors* 1 Itala *Max. B.H.P.* 40 *Capacity* 8,000 c.c. approx. *Ignition* L.T. magneto

TRANSMISSION *Clutch* Multi-plate *Gearbox* 4 speed and reverse *Final Drive* Shaft to bevel

DIMENSIONS, ETC.
Three seater *Length* 13 ft 6 ins *Width* 5 ft 6 ins *Wheelbase* 9 ft 7 ins *Tyre size* 735 × 135 *Average speed* 65 m.p.h. approx.

STANLEY EX 1907

The Stanley brothers started building steam cars in 1897. They designed a new, more modern car which became the 'Ex' in 1907. Special cars were built—the Teakettle, the Beetle, and the Rocket. Fred Marriot drove the Beetle at a speed of 121 m.p.h. Later at a speed of nearly 150 m.p.h. Marriot crashed and wrecked the car.

CHASSIS *Suspension (front)* Full elliptic springs *(rear)* Full elliptic springs *Brakes* Foot brake acts on band on differential casing. Handbrake acts on rear wheels only
ENGINE *Tank capacity* Water 26–35 galls. according to body *No. of Cyls.* 2 *Max. B.H.P.* 28 h.p.
TRANSMISSION *Clutch* None *Gearbox* None *Final Drive* Spur gear on crankshaft to toothed ring on differential
DIMENSIONS, ETC. *Wheelbase* 7 ft 6 ins *Tyre size* 30 × 3 *Weight* 12½ cwt

Henry Ford (1863–1947) built his first car in 1896 and started the Ford Motor Co. in 1903. The Model 'T' or 'Tin Lizzie' was the most famous of the early motor-cars. Cheap (at first $850, eventually $260), reliable, sturdily built and easy to maintain, it brought motoring to large numbers of people, and was in production for 18 years. Total sales amounted to 15 million. Production ended in 1927. The stories about the Model 'T' are legion and the car has passed into American country lore. Over 1,200 are restored and owned by enthusiasts in the U.S. today and many are owned and used in Rallies all over the world.

CHASSIS *Suspension (front)* Transverse ½ elliptic *(rear)* Transverse ½ elliptic
ENGINE 2.9 litre *Carburettors* 1 Holley *Capacity* 2,892 c.c. *No. of Cyls.* 4, side valve *Max. B.H.P.* 22 *Ignition* Flywheel magneto
DOORS 2
TRANSMISSION *Clutch* Multi-disc *Gearbox* 2 speed epicyclic *Final Drive* Shaft to bevel
DIMENSIONS, ETC.
Four seater *Length* 11 ft 4 ins *Width* 4 ft 8 ins *Wheelbase* 8 ft 4 ins *Tyre size* 30 × 3½ *Height* 6 ft 9 ins (hood up) *Weight* 13½ cwt *Top speed* 40–45 m.p.h.

OPEL
DOPPEL PHAETON
1908

The Opel car started when the Opel brothers in Germany built the Darracq car under licence. They then started designing cars of their own, and before long were building many of Germany's family cars. Opel went in for competitions, and just before the first World War produced racing cars with some success.

CHASSIS *Suspension (front)* ½ elliptic *(rear)* ½ elliptic *Brakes* Rear wheels only
ENGINE *No. of Cyls* 4 *Carburettors* 1 *Max. B.H.P.* 18 *Ignition* H.T. magneto
DOORS 2
TRANSMISSION *Clutch* Cone clutch *Gearbox* 3 speeds and reverse *Final Drive* Shaft to bevel gear
DIMENSIONS, ETC.
Four seater *Length* 12 ft 8 ins *Wheelbase* 9 ft 3 ins *Tyre size* 820 × 120 *Height* 7 ft 10 ins (hood up) *Average speed* 48 m.p.h. (approx.) max.

The Hupmobile was a small car designed to do much the same as the Model 'T' Ford, with which it was in direct competition. The 'Hup' was in some ways a better car—its performance was brisker—but it was not built in such massive numbers. Being light with a willing engine, the 'Hup' is a pleasant little car, typically American in many ways. The photo shows the only one left in Britain—restored from a few bits of rusty old iron the author obtained in Devon and sold to the present owner and restorer.

HUPMOBILE "20" called 12/14 in England 1909

CHASSIS *Suspension (front)* $\frac{1}{2}$ elliptic *(rear)* Transverse spring *Brakes* Rear wheels only
ENGINE *No. of Cyls.* 4 *Carburettors* 1 *Max. B.H.P.* 20 *Ignition* H.T. magneto
TRANSMISSION *Clutch* Multiple disk *Gearbox* 2 speed and reverse *Final Drive* Shaft to bevel gear
DIMENSIONS, ETC.
Two seater *Length* 10 ft 8 ins *Width* 5 ft approx. *Wheelbase* 8 ft 2 ins *Tyre size* 30 × 3$\frac{1}{2}$ *Weight* 12 cwt *Average speed* 50 m.p.h. max.

SWIFT
10/12
1909

The Swift Company started up in 1902, and soon established a reputation for good small cars. The earlier version of the 10/12 was successful in the Scottish Trials in 1907/8. This version, in production until 1912, was both reliable and pleasant to drive.

CHASSIS *Suspension (front)* $\frac{1}{2}$ elliptic *(rear)* $\frac{1}{2}$ elliptic *Brakes* Foot brake on the transmission Hand brake on rear wheels

ENGINE *No. of Cyls.* 2 *Carburettors* 1 Swift *Capacity* 1,800 c.c. *Ignition* H.T. magneto and trembler coil

TRANSMISSION *Clutch* Leather cone *Gearbox* 3 speed and reverse *Final Drive* Shaft

DIMENSIONS, ETC.
Two seater *Length* 11 ft 4 ins *Width* 5 ft 2 ins *Wheelbase* 7 ft 9 ins *Tyre size* 760 × 90 *Weight* 12 cwt *Average speed* 30/35 m.p.h.

We do not know much about the Russo-Baltique, built at Riga on orders from the Czar to make an all-Russian car. The car was based on the Belgian Fondu. It seems to have been quite a good car as it came third in the Riga—St. Petersburg—Riga race. Usually it had a 4-seater bodywork.

RUSSO-BALTIQUE
24/30
RACING
1909

CHASSIS *Suspension (front)* $\frac{1}{2}$ elliptic *(rear)* $\frac{1}{2}$ elliptic *Brakes* Rear wheels only
ENGINE *No. of Cyls.* 4 *Carburettors* 1 *Capacity* 4,800 c.c. *Ignition* H.T. magneto
TRANSMISSION *Gearbox* 3 speeds and reverse *Final Drive* Shaft to bevel gear
DIMENSIONS, ETC. Two seater

JOWETT
7 h.p.
1910

The Jowett was made in Bradford. The 2-cylinder engine was designed in 1910 and fitted to a light car which in various forms was in production until 1939. Our picture and details are of a 1925 car. The Jowett was a very popular economy car and the design, simple and even crude in places, lasted well. After the Second World War the Company made the 4-cylinder Javelin and Jupiter cars and the Bradford van with the 2-cylinder engine. Car production ceased in 1954.

CHASSIS *Suspension (front)* $\frac{1}{2}$ elliptic *(rear)* $\frac{1}{2}$ elliptic *Brakes* Rear wheels only
ENGINE *No. of Cyls.* 2 (flat twin) *Carburettors* 1 *Capacity* 826 c.c. *Ignition* H.T. magneto
DOORS 2
TRANSMISSION *Gearbox* 3 speeds and reverse *Final Drive* Shaft to bevel gear
DIMENSIONS, ETC.
Four seater *Length* 9 ft 9 ins *Wheelbase* 7 ft *Tyre size* 700 × 90 *Height* 5 ft (hood down) *Average speed* 50 m.p.h. approx. max.

Adler was one of the best known makes of car in Germany before the Second World War. Before the First World War, Adler's range of cars were very well made and designed, although technically conservative. In Germany, the Adler enjoyed a reputation roughly equivalent to that of Wolseley in England, although Adler was never very successful in motor sport until the introduction of their 'Trumf' f.w.d. cars in the early thirties.

CHASSIS *Suspension (front)* $\frac{1}{2}$ elliptic *(rear)* $\frac{1}{2}$ elliptic *Brakes* Foot—transmission Hand—rear wheels only
ENGINE *No. of Cyls.* 2 *Carburettors* 1 Adler *Max. B.H.P.* 8 *Ignition* H.T. magneto and trembler coil
TRANSMISSION *Clutch* Leather cone *Gearbox* 4 speed and reverse *Final Drive* Shaft to bevel gears
DIMENSIONS, ETC.
Two seater *Length* 12 ft 9 ins *Width* 4 ft 10 ins *Wheelbase* 9 ft 1 ins *Tyre size* 710 × 90 *Height* 5 ft 3 ins *Average speed* 45/50 m.p.h. max.

OLDSMOBILE LIMITED OPEN TOURER 1910

This Oldsmobile shows how quickly the firm changed its products from the curved dash model with one cylinder to a large car intended for the luxury customer. This car featured in a painting which became well known in America, of an Oldsmobile winning a race with an express train in 1910. It is typical of the expensive American car of 1910, although the electric head and side lamps combined is an unusual feature.

CHASSIS *Suspension (front)* $\frac{1}{2}$ elliptic *(rear)* $\frac{1}{2}$ elliptic *Brakes* Hand lever—internal on wheels Foot pedal—external on wheels
ENGINE
Tank capacity 22 galls. *No. of Cyls.* 6 in pairs *Carburettors* 1 *Max. B.H.P.* 60 *Ignition* H.T. magneto
BODY Pressed steel frame
DOORS 4
TRANSMISSION Selective *Clutch* Leather-faced cone
DIMENSIONS, ETC.
Length $15\frac{1}{2}$ ft *Width* 5 ft 5 ins *Wheelbase* 10 ft 10 ins *Tyre size* 42 × 5 *Height* 7 ft 7 ins (hood up) *Average speed* 75 m.p.h. max.

The Fiat Zero appeared at the end of 1912. It was the father of mass-produced Fiat cars. This car shows the lines of bodywork favoured from 1912 onwards, the sloping scuttle being typical of cars built from about 1912–1922.

FIAT "ZERO" TORPEDO 1912–1915

CHASSIS *Suspension (front)* $\frac{1}{2}$ elliptic *(rear)* $\frac{1}{2}$ elliptic *Brakes* Rear wheels only
ENGINE *Carburettors* 1 *Capacity* 1,846 c.c. *Max. B.H.P.* 19 *Ignition* H.T.
DOORS 4
TRANSMISSION *Clutch* Multiplate *Gearbox* 4 speed and reverse
DIMENSIONS, ETC.
Four seater *Length* 13 ft 3 ins Hood down *Wheelbase* 9 ft 6 ins *Tyre size* 760 × 90 *Weight* 900 kg *Average speed* 45 m.p.h.

PEUGEOT GRAND PRIX 1912

The 1912 Peugeot had a revolutionary twin overhead camshaft engine. It started the line of development of the high efficiency engine, through the 1923 Sunbeam down to the Jaguar XK engine. The photo shows Georges Boillot in the 1912 car in which he won the French Grand Prix. In the race it was painted, and had a stove guard in front of the radiator. Boillot also won the 1913 French Grand Prix in a Peugeot and came second in 1914 to Lantenschlager in a Mercedes.

CHASSIS *Suspension (front)* $\frac{1}{2}$ elliptic *(rear)* $\frac{1}{2}$ elliptic *Brakes* Rear wheels only
ENGINE *No. of Cyls.* 4 *Carburettors* 1 *Max. B.H.P.* 130 *Capacity* 7,602 c.c. *Ignition* H.T. magneto
TRANSMISSION *Gearbox* 4 speeds and reverse *Final Drive* Shaft to bevel gear
DIMENSIONS, ETC.
Two seater *Length* 9 ft 3$\frac{1}{2}$ ins *Width* 4 ft 10 ins *Average speed* 68 m.p.h.

Crossley cars were always very well constructed. Before the First World War they made a name for themselves in such rallies as the 1914 Swedish Winter Trials. The firm's name went into history when the R.F.C. used Crossley tenders with all its Squadrons serving in France. After the War the cars were continued until about 1935. There after the firm made buses and trolleybuses as part of the A.E.C. Group.

CROSSLEY "SHELSEY" OPEN TOURER 1913

CHASSIS *Suspension (front)* $\frac{1}{2}$ elliptic *(rear)* $\frac{1}{2}$ elliptic *Brakes* Foot—transmission Hand—rear wheels only
ENGINE *No. of Cyls.* 4 *Carburettors* 1 *Max. B.H.P.* 15 *Capacity* 2,600 c.c. approx. *Ignition* H.T. magneto
DOORS 3
TRANSMISSION *Clutch* Leather cone *Gearbox* 4 speed and reverse *Final Drive* Shaft to bevel gear
DIMENSIONS, ETC.
Four seater *Length* 12 ft *Wheelbase* 10 ft 4 ins *Tyre size* 820 × 120 *Average speed* 65 m.p.h. max.

PEUGEOT "BEBE" OPEN 1913

The Bébé was designed by Ettore Bugatti before he started his own company. It was the first real mini-car, as opposed to a single or twin-cylinder car or cycle-car. The Peugeot Bébé was popular in France as a touring car, used rather as the mini might be today.

CHASSIS *Suspension (front)* $\frac{1}{2}$ elliptic *(rear)* Reverse $\frac{1}{4}$ elliptic *Brakes* Rear wheel brakes only

ENGINE *No. of Cyls.* 4 *Carburettors* 1 *Max. B.H.P.* 10 *Capacity* 856 c.c. *Ignition* H.T. magneto

DOORS 1

TRANSMISSION *Gearbox* 3 speeds and reverse *Final Drive* Shaft to bevel gear

DIMENSIONS, ETC.
Two seater *Length* 7 ft 7 ins. *Width* 4 ft 11 ins *Weight* 8 cwt *Average speed* 48 m.p.h. max.

The Lagonda was built from 1910 onwards, most of the early cars being 11 h.p. and 20 h.p. The 11 h.p. model was continued until 1924. In the early years, most of the cars were exported to Russia, where they did well in Rallies. In the late twenties and early thirties, Lagonda made handsome sporting models, and in 1939 W. O. Bentley designed a V-12 4½ litre car for the company. Nowadays the Company, like Aston Martin, is part of the David Brown Group.

LAGONDA 11·9 h.p. OPEN TOURER 1913

CHASSIS *Suspension (front)* ½ elliptic *(rear)* ½ elliptic and radius rods

ENGINE *No. of Cyls.* 4 *Carburettors* 1 *Max. B.H.P.* 58 *Ignition* H.T. magneto

DOORS 4

TRANSMISSION *Clutch* Cone clutch *Gearbox* 3 speeds and reverse *Final Drive* Shaft to bevel gear

DIMENSIONS, ETC.
Four seater *Length* 11 ft 9 ins *Wheelbase* 9 ft 6 ins *Tyre size* 820 × 120 *Height* 4 ft 6 ins *Average speed* 65 m.p.h. approx. max.

VAUXHALL 30/98 "VELOX" OPEN TOURER 1913

Although the 30/98 is now considered one of the best Vintage sports cars made, it is really a light Edwardian touring car. The fact that it went so fast made many people think of it as a sports car. With a modified engine it won many competition successes. Nowadays a 30/98 fetches a very high price indeed.

CHASSIS *Suspension (front)* ½ elliptic *(rear)* ½ elliptic *Brakes* Foot brake transmission Hand brake rear wheels only

ENGINE *No. of Cyls.* 4 *Carburettors* 1 *Max. B.H.P.* 100 plus *Capacity* 4,300 c.c.

DOORS 3

TRANSMISSION *Clutch* Cone *Gearbox* 4 speeds and reverse
Final Drive Shaft to bevel gear

DIMENSIONS, ETC.
Four seater *Length* 13 ft 4 ins *Width* 5 ft 6 ins *Wheelbase* 9 ft 6 ins *Tyre size* 820 × 120 *Average speed* 85 m.p.h. with touring body

From the beginning of the century until just after World War I, Napier was one of the leading British makes. The firm was one of the first to build 6-cylinder motors, and continued to build large, powerful cars as long as it made cars. The example shown is somewhat small for Napier, but any Napier is rare and of interest. The bodywork is a fairly typical piece of late Edwardian luxury coachwork.

**NAPIER
30/35
TORPEDO 1913**

CHASSIS *Suspension (front)* Semi-elliptic *(rear)* $\frac{3}{4}$ elliptic *Brakes* Hand—rear Foot—transmission

ENGINE *Tank capacity* 14 galls. *No. of Cyls.* 6 *Carburettors* 1 Napier *Max. B.H.P.* 35 *Capacity* 4,750 c.c. *Ignition* H.T. magneto

DOORS 4

TRANSMISSION *Clutch* Dry plate *Gearbox* 3 speed and reverse *Final Drive* Open shaft to bevel gear

DIMENSIONS, ETC. Four seater *Length* 14 ft 9 ins *Tyre size* 895 × 135 *Height* 6 ft to screen *Weight* 24 cwt chassis only *Average speed* 50

BUGATTI
TYPE 13 "BRESCIA"
SPORTING 1914

Ettore Bugatti designed and produced his own 4-cylinder car in 1900, at the age of 19. In 1909 he set up as a manufacturer in a disused dye works near Strasbourg.

CHASSIS *Suspension (front)* Semi-elliptic *(rear)* Semi-elliptic After 1913 reversed quarter-elliptics *Brakes* Rear wheels only

ENGINE *Carburettors* 1 Zenith *Capacity* 1,496 c.c. *No. of Cyls.* 4 *Max. B.H.P.* 30 plus (touring cars) *Ignition* H.T. magneto

DOORS 2

TRANSMISSION *Clutch* Multiplate *Gearbox* 4 speeds and reverse *Final Drive* Bevel gear

DIMENSIONS, ETC.

Two seater *Length* 9 ft 9 ins to 10 ft 9 ins according to body work *Width* 4 ft 2 ins *Wheelbase* 3 ft 9 ins *Tyre size* 710 × 90 *Height* 3 ft 9 ins *Weight* 12 cwt *Average speed* 62 m.p.h. max.

This little car is typical of the light cars produced in Germany just before the First World War. It was, like all Adlers, nicely made, with a well-adjusted engine, although all pre-war Adlers tended to be rather conservative in design. The car in our picture was used in Kent until the mid-twenties and is still remembered with great affection by its original owner.

ADLER
11 h.p.
OPEN TOURER 1914

CHASSIS *Suspension (front)* ½ elliptic *Brakes* Foot transmission Hand rear wheels only **ENGINE** *No. of Cyls.* 4 *Carburettors* 1 Adler *Max. B.H.P.* 20 approx. *Capacity* 1,400 c.c. approx. *Ignition* H.T. magneto
DOORS 3
TRANSMISSION *Clutch* Cone *Gearbox* 4 speeds and reverse *Final Drive* Through tube to bevel gear
DIMENSIONS, ETC.
Four seater *Length* 11 ft *Wheelbase* 7 ft 10 ins *Tyre size* 760 × 90 *Height* 5 ft (hood down) *Weight* 15 cwt *Average speed* 45/50 m.p.h. max.

CHEVROLET ROYAL MAIL ROADSTER OPEN 1914

Louis Chevrolet first started making cars in 1912, when he made the Little, which looked similar to the Royal Mail Roadster, but was generally smaller. Chevrolet cars soon became popular and sold in large numbers. In 1917 a V-8 engine was introduced, and in 1923 Chevrolet introduced a short-lived air-cooled car. During the twenties Chevrolet became one of the top selling American cars.

CHASSIS *Suspension (front)* $\frac{1}{2}$ elliptic *(rear)* $\frac{3}{4}$ elliptic *Brakes* Rear wheels only
ENGINE *No. of Cyls.* 4 *Carburettors* 1 *Max. B.H.P.* 24 *Ignition* H.T. magneto
DOORS 2
TRANSMISSION *Gearbox* 3 speed and reverse *Final Drive* Shaft to bevel gear
DIMENSIONS, ETC.
Two seater *Length* 11 ft 8 ins *Wheelbase* 8 ft 8 ins *Tyre size* 30 × 3$\frac{1}{2}$ *Height* 5 ft (hood down) *Average speed* 50 m.p.h. approx. max.

DELAUNAY-BELLEVILLE OPEN TOURER 1914

The French considered the Delaunay-Belleville a match for the Rolls Royce. This firm had a long tradition of marine engineering before it started making cars. Soon it had a most impressive list of clients—the President of France, King Alfonso of Spain, the King of Greece and Tzar Nicholas, no less. The cars were usually large, beautifully built and carried a variety of coachwork. Our photo shows General Gallieni, organizer of the defence of Paris in August 1914, in an 'O' type.

CHASSIS *Suspension (front)* ½ elliptic *(rear)* ½ elliptic *Brakes* Two foot brakes on transmission (separate pedals) Hand brake on rear wheels only
ENGINE *No. of Cyls.* 6 *Carburettors* 1 Delaunay-Belleville *Max. B.H.P.* 50 *Capacity* 7,999 c.c. *Ignition* H.T. magneto
DOORS 3
TRANSMISSION *Clutch* Multidisk *Gearbox* 4 speed and reverse *Final Drive* Shaft to bevel gears
DIMENSIONS, ETC.
Four seater *Length* 16 ft 6 ins approx. *Width* 6 ft approx *Wheelbase* 11 ft 8 ins *Tyre size* 935 × 135 *Average speed* 75 m.p.h. approx.

FIAT
TIPO 501
1919

The Tipo 501 was introduced as a small family car. It was fitted with a complete electrical system and was well made. Some of the 4-seat open tourers were most attractive. Performance was not high but sufficient for the period. In 1925, the 501B was introduced, with four wheel brakes and balloon tyres. Production ceased in 1926.

CHASSIS *Suspension (front)* $\frac{1}{2}$ elliptic *(rear)* $\frac{1}{2}$ elliptic *Brakes* Foot—transmission Hand—rear wheels only
ENGINE *Tank capacity* 9 *No. of Cyls.* 4 *Carburettors* 1 Zenith *Max. B.H.P.* 15 *Capacity* 1,460 c.c.
TRANSMISSION *Clutch* Multidisk *Gearbox* 4 speed and reverse
DIMENSIONS, ETC.
Length 11 ft 3 ins (approx.) *Wheelbase* 8 ft $8\frac{1}{4}$ ins *Tyre size* 760 × 90 *Weight* 15 cwt (approx.) *Average speed* 50 m.p.h. max. (approx.)

Produced by Messrs. Godfrey & Nash originally in 1911, the G.N. was the most successful cycle car of the years before the war. Many different models were built, with different engines, carburettors, magnetos and body styles. Racing versions were successful in all forms of competition. The chain drive was used in the later Frazer-Nash. In the early twenties 4-cylinder engines were tried, but difficulties were encountered and the G.N. was no longer built after 1924.

CHASSIS *Suspension (front)* $\frac{1}{4}$ elliptic *(rear)* $\frac{1}{4}$ elliptic *Brakes* Rear wheels only
ENGINE *No. of Cyls.* V.2 *Carburettors* 1 *Max. B.H.P.* 22 *Capacity* 1,100 c.c. approx. *Ignition* H.T. magneto
DOORS 1
TRANSMISSION *Clutch* Single plate *Gearbox* 3 speed and reverse *Final Drive* Chain to solid axle (no diff.)
DIMENSIONS, ETC.
Two seater *Length* 11 ft 3 ins *Width* 4 ft 2 ins *Wheelbase* 8 ft 6 ins *Tyre size* 700 × 80 *Height* 5 ft 2 ins (hood up) *Weight* 8$\frac{1}{2}$ cwt *Average speed* 57 m.p.h. (max.)

MORRIS COWLEY SPORTS 1919

This photo shows William Morris in a rather unusual sports version of the extremely popular 'Bullnose' Morris. The standard version was built in thousands, and as the price was low, the car well-built, and the performance good for the size of the car, it was an excellent buy. The Morris, together with Herbert Austin's Seven, were to Englishmen what the Model 'T' was to Americans.

CHASSIS *Suspension (front)* $\frac{1}{2}$ elliptic *(rear)* $\frac{1}{2}$ elliptic *Brakes* Rear wheels only Front wheel brake extra 1926 **ENGINE** *Tank capacity* 5 *Carburettors* 1 (various makes according to year) *Capacity* 1,548 c.c. *No. of Cyls.* 4 *Max. B.H.P.* 26 *Ignition* H.T. magneto **DOORS** 1 **TRANSMISSION** *Clutch* 2 driven plates *Gearbox* 3 speed and reverse *Final Drive* Tongue tube and spiral bevel **STEERING** Worm and wheel **DIMENSIONS, ETC.** *Length* 11 ft 4 ins *Width* 4 ft 8 ins *Wheelbase* 8 ft 6 ins *Height* 4 ft 8 ins (hood down) *Average speed* 50/55 max.

The Bean, a good solid family car, was built by the old firm of A. Harper Sons & Bean. The photo shows a 1926 car once owned by the author. The Bean was soundly built and though its performance was not what it might have been, it *did* last! In 1927 a Bean driven by Francis Birtles went from London to Melbourne.

**BEAN
12 h.p.
TOURER 1920**

CHASSIS *Suspension (front)* $\frac{1}{2}$ elliptic *(rear)* $\frac{1}{2}$ elliptic *Brakes* Rear wheels only
ENGINE *No. of Cyls.* 4 *Carburettors* 1 *Max. B.H.P.* 12 *Capacity* 1800 c.c. approx. *Ignition* Magneto
DOORS 4
TRANSMISSION *Clutch* Dry plate *Gearbox* 4 speed and reverse *Final Drive* Shaft to bevel gear
DIMENSIONS, ETC.
Four seater *Length* 12 ft 8 ins (hood down) *Width* 5 ft 7 ins *Wheelbase* 8 ft 6 ins *Tyre size* 450 × 19 *Height* 5 ft 8 ins (hood down) *Average speed* 55 m.p.h. max.

MORGAN GRAND PRIX 1920

During the years immediately before and after the First World War many cycle cars and three-wheelers were built, but the only one to experience popularity was the Morgan. It had its faults, but its performance appealed to the sporting motorist just as present-day Morgans do. Various engines by J.A.P., Precision, or M.A.G. were fitted, either air or water cooled. In the thirties, the Morgan became a 4-wheel car and, with more powerful engines fitted, hasn't changed much since.

CHASSIS *Suspension (front)* Independent coil springs *(rear)* $\frac{1}{4}$ elliptic *Brakes* Rear wheels only

ENGINE *No. of Cyls.* 2 *Carburettors* 1 *Max. B.H.P.* 8 h.p. (rated) *Capacity* 1,000 c.c. (according to engine) *Ignition* Magneto

TRANSMISSION *Clutch* Dog clutches *Gearbox* 2 speed, no reverse *Final Drive* Chain

DIMENSIONS, ETC

Two seater *Length* 9 ft *Wheelbase* 6 ft *Tyre size* 700 × 80 *Height* 4 ft (hood up) *Weight* 4 cwt approx. *Average speed* 65 m.p.h.

The Storey was a typical product of the Car Boom after the First World War. It was built at first in London, then, when the factory was finished, at Tonbridge in Kent. Fourteen and twenty h.p. cars were built. Standard bodies were the Tonbridge saloon, the London Coupé, the Kent Tourer and the Kent 2 seater. The total number of Storey's built was about 1,500.

CHASSIS *Suspension (front)* $\frac{1}{2}$ elliptic *(rear)* $\frac{1}{2}$ elliptic *Brakes* Rear wheels only
ENGINE *No. of Cyls.* 4 *Carburettors* 1 Zenith *Ignition* H.T. Magneto
TRANSMISSION *Clutch* Cone clutch *Gearbox* 3 speeds and reverse *Final Drive* Tongue tube to overhead worm gear
DIMENSIONS, ETC.
Length 14 ft 4 ins *Wheelbase* 10 ft 8 ins *Tyre size* 820 × 120

MERCER
22-70
RACEABOUT
1921

In America, from about 1910 until the early twenties, there were only two *real* sports cars, the Stutz and the Mercer, and the loyalty to one make or the other which existed then has continued to this day. A car of either make will fetch a very high price indeed. The design of both cars tended to be conservative, but the cars, both Stutz and Mercer, were beautifully made, and the handling and roadholding were up to the best European standards—unusual in American cars of the period.

CHASSIS *Suspension (front)* $\frac{1}{2}$ elliptic *(rear)* $\frac{1}{2}$ elliptic *Brakes* Rear wheels only
ENGINE *Tank capacity* 25 galls. *No. of Cyls.* 4 *Carburettors* 1 *Max B.H.P.* 70 *Capacity* 4,900 c.c. approx. *Ignition* H.T. magneto
TRANSMISSION *Gearbox* 4 speed and reverse *Final Drive* Shaft
DIMENSIONS, ETC.
Two seater *Length* 11 ft 11 ins *Wheelbase* 9 ft 7 ins (or 11 ft) *Tyre size* 32 x $4\frac{1}{2}$ *Height* 4 ft $11\frac{1}{2}$ ins *Weight* $22\frac{1}{4}$ cwt *Average speed* 80 m.p.h. max. (approx.)

The Type 513 was Fiat's luxury car built in the early twenties, the idea being to try to capture some of the luxury car market in America. The type 513 was only built for two years, so it seems reasonable to suppose that it did not appeal to the Americans much more than their own types. After the First World War, the Americans were not as keen to import cars as they had been, preferring home-built cars.

**FIAT
513
COUPE DE VILLE
1922**

CHASSIS *Suspension (front)* $\frac{1}{2}$ elliptic *(rear)* $\frac{1}{2}$ elliptic *Brakes* Rear wheels only
ENGINE *No. of Cyls.* 6 *Carburettors* 1 *Max. B.H.P.* 77 *Capacity* 4,766 *Ignition* H.T. magneto
DOORS 4
TRANSMISSION *Clutch* Multidisk *Gearbox* 4 speed and reverse *Final Drive* Shaft to bevel gears
DIMENSIONS, ETC.
Six seater *Length* 16 ft 3 ins *Width* 5 ft 9 ins *Wheelbase* 11 ft 10 ins *Tyre size* 895 × 135 *Height* 6 ft 2 ins *Average speed* 70 m.p.h. max. (approx.)

LANCIA "LAMBDA" OPEN TORPEDO 1922

The Lambda was introduced in 1922 and was intended as a four seat tourer. Its construction was unusual, with independent front suspension, narrow V engine and a monocoque hull to which all the mechanical parts were fitted. The body and mudguards were fitted to this hull also. The Lambda had a style of its own which was rather attractive. Some of the saloon cars had wickerwork front seats.

CHASSIS *Suspension (front)* Independent suspension with coil springs *(rear)* $\frac{1}{2}$ elliptic *Brakes* 4 wheel
ENGINE *Tank capacity* 13 galls. *No. of Cyls.* 4 *Carburettors* 1 Zenith *Max. B.H.P.* 48 *Capacity* 2,125 c.c. *Ignition* H.T. magneto
DOORS 4
TRANSMISSION *Clutch* Plate *Gearbox* 3 speed and reverse. Later version had 4 speeds *Final Drive* Shaft to bevel gear
DIMENSIONS, ETC.
Four seater *Length* 14 ft 4 ins *Width* 4 ft $5\frac{1}{4}$ ins *Wheelbase* 10 ft 2 ins *Tyre size* 765 × 105 *Height* 5 ft 5 ins (hood up) *Weight* 23 cwt *Average speed* 70/75 m.p.h. max.

The Trojan Utility was designed by Leslie Houndslow and the first car was built in 1910, but serious production did not start until Leyland built the Trojan under licence. The Trojan was intended as a cheap people's car, rather like the Ford Model 'T'. It was very popular and sold in large numbers. It was unconventional in almost every way, having a 2-stroke engine, solid tyres and an epicyclic gearbox.

TROJAN "UTILITY" OPEN TOURER 1922

CHASSIS *Suspension (front)* Cantilever leaf springs *(rear)* Cantilever leaf springs *Brakes* Rear wheels only
ENGINE *No. of Cyls.* 4 (2 stroke) *Carburettors* 1 *Max. B.H.P.* 11 *Capacity* 1,529 c.c. (1923 onwards 1,488 c.c.) *Ignition* H.T. coil
DOORS 3
TRANSMISSION *Clutch* 2 hand brakes in gear box *Gearbox* 2 speed and reverse (epicyclic) *Final Drive* Chain, no differential fitted
DIMENSIONS, ETC.
Four seater *Length* 10 ft 6 ins *Width* 4 ft 9 ins *Wheelbase* 8 ft *Tyre size* Solids 28 × 2½ (Pneumatic 710 × 90) *Height* 5 ft 11 ins *Average speed* 25 m.p.h.

AUSTIN TWELVE OPEN TOURER 1922

The Austin 12 was one of the best made cars of its type. The performance was low but the car lasted on and on, and the design was modified for London Taxis, which also lasted indefinitely. The Austin range at the time was the Seven, Twelve, the 16 h.p. and the 20 h.p. The Seven and the Twelve were the best sellers in the range. Saloon and two-seater versions were also built, but the tourer was the most popular and was well known for its durability and good finish.

CHASSIS *Suspension (front)* ½ elliptic *(rear)* ½ elliptic *Brakes* Rear wheels only
ENGINE *No. of Cyls.* 4 *Carburettors* 1 Zenith *Capacity* 1,661 c.c. *Ignition* Magneto
DOORS 4
TRANSMISSION *Clutch* Plate *Gearbox* 4 speeds and reverse *Final Drive* Shaft to bevel gear
DIMENSIONS, ETC.
Four seater *Length* 13 ft 2 ins *Wheelbase* 9 ft 4 ins *Tyre size* 765 × 105 *Average speed* 50 m.p.h. max.

The Austin Seven was designed to replace the cycle cars and motor cycle combinations that were the only cheap transport in the early twenties. It too was cheap and, with the very low fuel consumption, the running costs were negligible. The Seven sold well and production went on, in various forms, until the Baby went out of production in 1938. Most of the coach builders built bodies on the Austin Seven at one time or another, and it became a very successful sports and racing car.

CHASSIS *Suspension (front)* Transverse half elliptic *(rear)* Quarter elliptic *Brakes* 4 wheel. Hand brake to front wheels. Foot brake to rear.
ENGINE *Tank capacity* 4 galls *No. of Cyls.* 4 *Carburettors* 1 Zenith *Max. B.H.P.* 10.5 (rated h.p.) *Capacity* 7.47 c.c. *Ignition* H.T. magneto
DOORS 2
TRANSMISSION *Clutch* Single dry plate *Gearbox* 3 speed and reverse *Final Drive* Torque tube and bevel gear
DIMENSIONS, ETC.
Two seater *Length* 8 ft 10 ins *Width* 3 ft 10 ins *Wheelbase* 6 ft 3 ins *Tyre size* 26 × 3 *Weight* 7 cwt *Average speed* 40 m.p.h. max.

CLYNO
11 h.p. "ROYAL"
TOURER
1923/4

In the middle twenties the Clyno was one of the three top selling British cars. It was a very popular family car, made either as a four seat open tourer, a two seater with a 'dicky' seat, a saloon, and later on a van. In 1928 a 9 h.p. car was introduced. The company went bankrupt in September 1929. Nowadays the Clyno is quite rare but at one time, in the middle twenties, production ran at about 225 per week. The Clyno was one of the first cheap cars to have four wheel brakes and balloon tyres.

CHASSIS *Suspension (front)* $\frac{1}{4}$ elliptic later $\frac{1}{2}$ elliptic *(rear)* $\frac{1}{4}$ elliptic later $\frac{1}{2}$ elliptic *Brakes* Rear wheels only (1925 four wheel brakes)
ENGINE *No. of Cyls.* 4 *Carburettors* 1 *Max. B.H.P.* 25 plus *Capacity* 1,368 c.c. *Ignition* H.T. magneto
DOORS 3
TRANSMISSION *Clutch* Single plate *Gearbox* 3 speed and reverse *Final Drive* Shaft to bevel gear
DIMENSIONS, ETC.
Four seater *Length* 11 ft 7 ins *Wheelbase* 8 ft 9 ins *Weight* 14 cwt

This is one of the later Model 'T's as used in the U.S. and in Britain. The finish was still black and a choice of colour was reinstated in the last year or so of the production run. Wire wheels also appeared in the last year but the design was then many years out of date and it was only the price that kept production going. In 1927 production ceased and the Model 'T' was replaced by the new Model 'A'.

FORD "T" SALOON 1923

CHASSIS *Suspension (front)* Transverse $\frac{1}{2}$ elliptic *(rear)* Transverse $\frac{1}{2}$ elliptic *Brakes* Rear wheels only
ENGINE *No. of Cyls.* 4 *Carburettors* 1 Holley *Max. B.H.P.* 20 *Capacity* 2,900 c.c. *Ignition* Flywheel magneto
DOORS 4
TRANSMISSION *Clutch* Multidisk clutch for high gear *Gearbox* Low gear and reverse bands on gear drums *Final Drive* Torque tube to bevel gears
DIMENSIONS, ETC.
Four seater *Length* 11 ft 4 ins *Width* 5 ft 4 ins *Wheelbase* 8 ft 4 ins *Tyre size* 30 × 3$\frac{1}{2}$ *Height* 6 ft *Average speed* 28–35 m.p.h.

RENAULT
8 h.p. SALOON
1923

The Renault 8 h.p. was one of a range of cars built by the company during the twenties designed to appeal to people requiring a small car, cheap to buy and to run. It achieved great popularity, and can still be seen on the roads of France.

CHASSIS *Suspension (front)* ½ elliptic *Brakes* Rear wheels only

ENGINE *No. of Cyls.* 4 *Carburettors* 1 *Max. B.H.P.* 20 approx. *Capacity* 1,000 c.c. *Ignition* H.T. magneto

DOORS 4

TRANSMISSION *Gearbox* 3 speed and reverse *Final Drive* Shaft to bevel gear

DIMENSIONS, ETC.
Four seater *Length* 10 ft 8 ins *Wheelbase* 8 ft *Tyre size* 700 × 80 *Height* 5 ft 4 ins *Weight* 15 cwt approx. *Average speed* 45/50 m.p.h. max.

ALFA-ROMEO
1924 P2/1932 P3

The Alfa-Romeo racing cars of the twenties and thirties achieved fantastic successes. The cars were designed by a man named Jans who had been 'pinched' from Fiat to head the design team at Ferrari's suggestion. The cars raced long after the time when they became overshadowed by Auto-Union and Mercedes-Benz, but handled by such brilliant drivers as Varzi and the famous Navolari they won races long after they should have been retired.

CHASSIS *Suspension (front)* $\frac{1}{2}$ elliptic *(rear)* $\frac{1}{2}$ elliptic *Brakes* 4 wheel brakes
ENGINE *Tank capacity* 32 galls. *No. of Cyls.* 8 *Carburettors* 2 Nemini and supercharger *Max. B.H.P.* 175 *Capacity* 1,987 c.c. *Ignition* Magneto
BODY *Type* Grand Prix *Seating* 2 (P2); 1 (P3)
TRANSMISSION *Clutch* Multidisk *Gearbox* 4 speed and reverse *Final Drive* Tongue tube bevel gear
DIMENSIONS, ETC.
Length 12 ft 7 ins *Width* 5 ft *Wheelbase* 8 ft 7 ins *Tyre size* 29 × 5.50 *Height* 3 ft 9 ins *Weight* 15$\frac{1}{2}$ cwt with spare wheel (dry) *Average speed* 120 m.p.h. plus max. (P2)

ALVIS
12/50
"DUCKS BACK"
1924

The Alvis company was started after the First World War and their 12/30 model was a moderate success. When it was given overhead valves it became the 12/50. This was intended as a four seat tourer, but with two seat sports bodies they started to win competitions all over the country and were extremely successful. Since then, they have kept their popularity, so that today they are considered typical Vintage sports cars.

CHASSIS *Suspension (front)* $\frac{1}{2}$ elliptic *(rear)* $\frac{1}{2}$ elliptic *Brakes* 4 wheel
ENGINE *No. of Cyls.* 4 *Carburettors* 1 *Max. B.H.P.* 53 *Capacity* 1,643 c.c. *Ignition* H.T. magneto
DOORS 1
TRANSMISSION *Clutch* Cone replaced by single plate 1926 *Gearbox* 4 speed and reverse *Final Drive* Shaft to bevel gear
DIMENSIONS, ETC.
Two seater *Length* 12 ft (approx.) *Wheelbase* 9 ft $\frac{1}{2}$ in *Tyre size* 28 × 3$\frac{1}{2}$ *Height* 4 ft 9 ins *Weight* 9$\frac{1}{2}$ cwt *Average speed* 75 m.p.h.

The O.M. was built in Italy as a fast touring car and quickly became popular in Britain amongst sporting motorists who used it with considerable success. It was a beautifully built car, if somewhat noisy, and it certainly went better than one would expect from the size of the engine. It was fitted with a large comfortable body. O.M. ceased making cars in 1933 when Mussolini ordered the factory to make lorries for the Italian Army.

O.M. 14/45 TORPEDO 1924

CHASSIS *Suspension (front)* $\frac{1}{2}$ elliptic *(rear)* $\frac{1}{2}$ elliptic *Brakes* 4 wheel brakes

ENGINE *Tank capacity* 17 galls *No. of Cyls.* 6 *Carburettors* 1 Zenith *Max. B.H.P.* 45 *Capacity* 1,991 c.c.

DOORS 4

TRANSMISSION *Clutch* Steel disk *Gearbox* 4 speed and reverse *Final Drive* Shaft to spiral bevel

DIMENSIONS, ETC.

Four seater *Length* 13 ft 10 ins *Wheelbase* 10 ft 2 ins *Tyre size* 765 × 105 *Height* 5 ft 9 ins (hood down) *Weight* 36 cwt *Average speed* 50/55 m.p.h. cruising speed

SWIFT "Q" OPEN TOURER 1924

The Swift was a 10 h.p. family car that was quite well made although the design was not very exciting and the performance rather low. They were popular however, and sold well. These pleasant little cars had fair brakes and fantastic steering. In 1927 the car was fitted with a 4 speed gearbox which helped performance and 4 wheel brakes which ruined the steering, which became less sensitive. A 12 h.p. car was also built in smaller numbers. Production ceased in 1932. The author has had 3 of these cars and they were all great fun.

CHASSIS *Suspension (front)* $\frac{1}{4}$ elliptic *(rear)* $\frac{1}{4}$ elliptic *Brakes* Rear wheels only
ENGINE *Tank capacity* 5 galls. approx. *No. of Cyls.* 4 *Carburettors* 1 Solex *Max. B.H.P.* 10 *Capacity* 1,097 c.c. *Ignition* H.T. magneto
DOORS 3
TRANSMISSION *Clutch* Single dry plate *Gearbox* 3 speed and reverse *Final Drive* Shaft to bevel gears
DIMENSIONS, ETC.
Four seater *Length* 11 ft 9 ins *Width* 4 ft 6 ins *Wheelbase* 8 ft 3 ins *Tyre size* 4.50 × 19 *Height* 5 ft 8 ins (Hood up) *Weight* 15 cwt *Average speed* 45 m.p.h. (max.)

RILEY 9 1926

The Riley 9 was the first small car with a high performance produced in Britain for a fairly low price. The saloon '9' could do 60 m.p.h. whereas the Austin 12 could only manage about 50 m.p.h. The Riley became very popular with sporting drivers and was developed into the famous Riley 12 series, so popular in the thirties. Names like 'Monaco', 'Merlin', 'Imp' and 'Kestrel' are all connected with Riley's of this period, and any car of this type is a collector's piece today. They were well made, and all performed well.

CHASSIS *Suspension (front)* $\frac{1}{2}$ elliptic *(rear)* $\frac{1}{2}$ elliptic *Brakes* 4 wheel brakes
ENGINE *Tank capacity* 5 galls *No. of Cyls.* 4 *Carburettors* 1 Zenith *Max. B.H.P.* 29 *Capacity* 1,110 c.c. *Ignition* H.T. magneto
DOORS 4
TRANSMISSION *Clutch* Cone plate later *Gearbox* 4 speeds and reverse *Final Drive* Torque tube to spiral bevel
DIMENSIONS, ETC.
Four seater *Length* 12 ft 5 ins *Width* 4 ft 9 ins *Wheelbase* 9 ft *Tyre size* 27 × 4.40 *Weight* 17 cwt *Average speed* About 60 m.p.h. max.

DAIMLER 35/120 OPEN TOURER 1928

The Royal Family bought Daimlers from the beginning of the century and from 1908 these luxurious cars used sleeve valves in their large engines. The cars were usually large, high and very luxurious, silent but with very little performance and quite a thirst for petrol and oil. They were beautifully made, however, and deserve a better fate than many of them have received—ending up at the car breakers. After the Second World War, the cars became smaller with a higher performance. Our photo shows a rather rare open tourer.

CHASSIS *Suspension (front)* $\frac{1}{2}$ elliptic *(rear)* $\frac{1}{2}$ elliptic *Brakes* 4 wheel brakes
ENGINE *No. of Cyls.* 6 *Carburettors* 1 *Max. B.H.P.* 120 *Capacity* 5,764 c.c. *Ignition* Coil and magneto
DOORS 4
TRANSMISSION *Clutch* Disk *Gearbox* 4 speeds and reverse *Final Drive* Shaft to bevel gear
DIMENSIONS, ETC.
Four seater *Length* 15 ft 7 ins *Wheelbase* 12 ft 4 ins *Tyre size* 33 × 6.75 *Height* 5 ft 6 ins (hood down)

HISPANO-SUIZA "BOULOGNE" SPORTS TOURER 1928

The firm of Hispano-Suiza built cars in France and Spain and they were among the best cars ever made.

Before the First World War their best known car was the $3\frac{1}{2}$ litre 'Alfonso' model, named after King Alfonso XIII, who drove at least one car of this type. After the War the cars became bigger, with an advanced design. During the twenties and early thirties the Hispano-Suiza was 'the' car for the sporting young man-about-town.

CHASSIS *Suspension (front)* $\frac{1}{2}$ elliptic *(rear)* $\frac{1}{2}$ elliptic *Brakes* 4 wheel brakes servo-operated

ENGINE *No. of Cyls.* 6 *Carburettors* 1 *Max. B.H.P.* 100 *Capacity* 3,800 c.c. *Ignition* H.T. magneto

DOORS 4

TRANSMISSION *Gearbox* 3 speeds and reverse

DIMENSIONS, ETC. Four seater *Length* 16 ft approx. (according to body style) *Width* 5 ft 10 ins *Wheelbase* 11 ft *Tyre size* 895 × 135 *Height* 5 ft 4 ins *Average speed* 100 m.p.h. plus

DELAGE
D.8 SPORTS SALOON
1929

The D.8 was the last of a long line of high performance cars built by this French firm, which, unfortunately, went bankrupt after the slump of 1929. The D.8 series was continued as a luxury sporting car throughout the thirties. The last of the series was the D.8.120, which had i.f.s. and the fabulous electric Cotal gearbox.

CHASSIS *Suspension (front)* $\frac{1}{2}$ elliptic *(rear)* $\frac{1}{2}$ elliptic *Brakes* 4 wheel brakes. Drum **ENGINE** *No. of Cyls.* 8 *Carburettors* 1 *Max. B.H.P.* 110 h.p. *Capacity* 4,000 c.c. approx.
DOORS 4
TRANSMISSION *Clutch* Single dry plate *Gearbox* 4 speeds and reverse *Final Drive* Shaft to bevel gears
DIMENSIONS, ETC.
Four seater *Length* 15 ft 6 ins *Wheelbase* 10 ft 10 ins or 11 ft 11 ins *Tyre size* 7 × 20 *Height* 5 ft 10 ins approx.

During the twenties the Crossley range of cars was more notable for finish and durability than performance. Towards the end of the decade Crossley followed the six cylinder fashion that was prevalent in the Motor Industry and the cars lost their appeal. In 1932 a series of cheap family cars appeared, but were not a success. Crossley engines were fitted to some Lagondas.

CROSSLEY 15.7 h.p. FABRIC SALOON 1929

CHASSIS *Suspension (front)* $\frac{1}{2}$ elliptic *(rear)* $\frac{1}{2}$ elliptic *Brakes* 4 wheel brakes
ENGINE *No. of Cyls.* 6 *Carburettors* 1 *Capacity* 2,700 c.c.
DOORS 2
TRANSMISSION *Clutch* Disk *Gearbox* 4 speeds and reverse *Final Drive* Shaft to bevel gear
DIMENSIONS, ETC.
Four seater *Length* 11 ft 4 ins *Wheelbase* 10 ft 5 ins *Tyre size* 820 × 120 *Height* 5 ft 10 ins *Average speed* 70 m.p.h. max. (approx.)

BENTLEY
4½ LITRE
OPEN TOURER 1929

For many people the 'Blower Bentley'—the supercharged 4½ litre car—is the ultimate sports car. Developed by Sir Henry Birkin, one of the 'Bentley Boys', the car was used in some of the top competition events of the period, including Le Mans. At the French Grand Prix in 1930 Bentley came in second, running against single seat G.P. racing cars. No wonder Bugatti called them 'the fastest lorries in Europe'!

CHASSIS *Suspension (front)* ½ elliptic *(rear)* ½ elliptic *Brakes* Drums on all wheels
ENGINE *Tank capacity* 16 galls. *No. of Cyls.* 4 *Carburettors* 2 S.U.'s *Max. B.H.P.* 240 *Capacity* 4,398 c.c. *Ignition* 2 magnetos
DOORS 3
TRANSMISSION *Clutch* Disk *Gearbox* 4 speed and reverse *Final Drive* Shaft to bevel gear
DIMENSIONS, ETC.
Four seater *Length* 14 ft 7 ins *Width* 5 ft 8½ ins *Wheelbase* 10 ft 10 ins *Tyre size* 600 × 21 *Height* 4 ft 8 ins *Weight* 34 cwt *Average speed* 125 m.p.h. max.

The Austin Swallow was one of the many variants of the Seven that became so popular in the late twenties and early thirties. The cars of Swallow Sidecars Ltd. were rather racier than many. They also built bodies on Swifts and one or two of the light cars of the period. They were obviously successful because they built the Swallow Standard or S.S. which developed into the Jaguar that we know today.

AUSTIN SWALLOW SALOON 1930

CHASSIS *Suspension (front)* Transverse $\frac{1}{2}$ elliptic *(rear)* $\frac{1}{4}$ elliptic *Brakes* Hand and foot operated on 4 wheels
ENGINE *No. of Cyls.* 4 *Carburettors* 1 Zenith *Max. B.H.P.* 10.5 *Capacity* 747.5 c.c. *Ignition* Coil
DOORS 2
TRANSMISSION *Clutch* Single dry plate *Gearbox* 3 speeds and reverse *Final Drive* Torque tube and bevel gear
DIMENSIONS, ETC.
Four seater *Length* 9 ft 10 ins *Width* 4 ft 1 in *Wheelbase* 6 ft 3 ins *Tyre size* 26 × 3 *Height* 5 ft 1 in *Weight* 7 cwt approx. *Average speed* 55 max. (approx.)

WOLSELEY HORNET 1930

The Wolseley 'Hornet' introduced in 1930 was produced for 5 years. In this time many were sold and specialist body builders fitted bodies of their own designs—two seaters, four seaters and even some saloons. The Hornet was a typical inexpensive sports car of the thirties, yet lavishly equipped for the price charged. It did well in competitions, often against much more expensive cars. Nowadays a Hornet is a car worth getting.

CHASSIS *Suspension (front)* ½ elliptic *(rear)* ½ elliptic *Brakes* Hydraulic 4 wheel brakes

ENGINE *No. of Cyls.* 6 *Carburettors* 2 S.U.'s *Max. B.H.P.* 40 *Capacity* 1,271 c.c. (later 1,604 c.c.)

DOORS 2

TRANSMISSION *Clutch* Single plate *Gearbox* 4 speed and reverse *Final Drive* Shaft to bevel gear

DIMENSIONS, ETC.
Four seater *Length* 10 ft 6 ins —11 ft according to body etc. *Wheelbase* 7 ft 6 ins—7 ft 11 ins *Tyre size* 4.75 × 19, later 500 × 18 *Weight* 15—18 cwt depending on body *Average speed* 75 m.p.h. max.

This car was based on the Morris 'Minor' of 1928 and it had the same three speed gearbox. The fabric body fitted to many of the cars kept them light and the performance was better than one might have expected, the top speed of the production model being about 65 m.p.h. From this car came the long line of M.G. 'Midgets', types 'P' and 'T'.

MORRIS MINOR SALOON 1930

CHASSIS *Suspension (front)* Semi-elliptic leaf springs *(rear)* Semi-elliptic leaf springs *Brakes* 4 wheel brakes
ENGINE *Tank capacity* 5 galls. *Carburettors* 1 S.U. *Capacity* 847 c.c. *No. of Cyls.* 4 *Max. B.H.P.* 20 @ 3,500 *Ignition* Coil
DOORS 2
TRANSMISSION *Clutch* Borg & Beck single dry plate *Gearbox* 3 speed and reverse *Final Drive* Shaft to spiral bevel
DIMENSIONS, ETC.
Length 10 ft 1 in *Width* 4 ft 2 ins *Wheelbase* 6 ft 6 ins *Tyre size* 27 × 4 *Height* 5 ft 3 ins *Weight* 11¾ cwt *Average speed* 60 m.p.h. max. (approx.)

RENAULT SPEED MODEL FIXED HEAD COUPE 1931

This car is rather typical of the French car of the thirties; the bodywork was stylish without being ostentatious. The large luggage trunk is interesting. This fitting was popular in the thirties and somehow looks more rakish than the later 'boot'.

CHASSIS *Suspension (front)* Semi-elliptic *(rear)* Transverse *Brakes* 4 wheel. H/brake rear only
ENGINE *Tank capacity* 8 galls. *No. of Cyls.* 4 *Carburettors* Zenith *Capacity* 2,120 c.c. *Ignition* Coil
DOORS 2 (Fixed Head Coupé), 4 (Saloon)
TRANSMISSION *Clutch* Dry single disc *Gearbox* 3 forward, 1 reverse, Synchromesh *Final Drive* Spiral bevel
DIMENSIONS, ETC.
Four–five seater *Length* 13 ft 10 ins *Width* 5 ft 2 ins *Wheelbase* 8 ft 8 ins *Tyre size* 17 × 5 *Height* 5 ft 8 ins

This handsome car was an M.G. design throughout, except for using a modified Morris 'Isis' engine. Originally produced as the MK1 in 1928, this had a rather flexible chassis with a 3 speed gearbox. The MK11 was slightly slower but was considered a better car. From this the M.G. 'Magnette' gradually evolved.

**M.G.
SIX TOURER MK 11
1932**

CHASSIS *Suspension (front)* ½ elliptic *(rear)* ½ elliptic *Brakes* 4 wheel brakes
ENGINE *Tank capacity* 6 galls. *No. of Cyls.* 6 *Carburettors* 2 S.U. *Max B.H.P.* 37.2 *Capacity* 2,400 c.c.
DOORS 2
TRANSMISSION *Clutch* Single dry plate *Gearbox* 4 speed C type, non-synchromesh *Final Drive* Shaft
DIMENSIONS, ETC.
Four seater *Length* 13 ft 8 ins *Wheelbase* 9 ft 6 ins *Tyre size* 29 × 5 *Weight* 15 cwt *Average speed* 80 m.p.h. max.

FIAT
TIPO 508
DROPHEAD COUPE
1932–34

The Fiat 508 was a small family car, with a dickey seat, similar in appearance to the Model 'A' Ford introduced a few years earlier. Other body types were available, and this car held roughly the same position in the Italian market as the Swift 10 or the Austin 10 in Britain.

CHASSIS *Suspension (front)* ½ elliptic *(rear)* ½ elliptic
ENGINE *No. of Cyls.* 4 *Carburettors* 1 *Max. B.H.P.* 20 *Capacity* 995 c.c. *Ignition* Coil
DOORS 2
TRANSMISSION *Clutch* Multi disc *Gearbox* 3 speed and reverse *Final Drive* Shaft to bevel gear
DIMENSIONS, ETC.
Two seater *Length* 11 ft 5 ins *Width* 4 ft 7 ins *Wheelbase* 7 ft 4 ins *Tyre size* 400 × 17 *Height* 5 ft *Weight* 18 cwt *Average speed* 60 m.p.h. (max.)

The Auto Union P-Wagon was designed by Dr. Porsche, and although it was similar to the 1923 Mercedes-Benz, when it appeared it was considered revolutionary. The handling was tricky but even so the cars were successful, and, with the Mercedes-Benz cars built at the same time, made Germany supreme in Grand Prix racing from 1934 to 1939. The success of the Auto Union probably did much to make designers think of the rear engine layout for cars, as they proved the possibility of this type.

AUTO UNION GRAND PRIX 1933 (1936 shown)

CHASSIS *Suspension (front)* Independent, torsion bars *(rear)* Independent, torsion bars *Brakes* 4 wheel brakes, hydraulic
ENGINE *Tank capacity* 46 galls. *No. of Cyls.* 16 *Carburettors* 2 Solex (Supercharged) *Max. B.H.P.* 520 *Capacity* 6,010 c.c. *Ignition* 2 magnetos
TRANSMISSION *Clutch* Multi-plate *Gearbox* 4 speed and reverse *Final Drive* Shaft to bevel gear
DIMENSIONS, ETC.
Length 12 ft 9 ins *Width* 5 ft 6 ins *Wheelbase* 9 ft 6 ins *Tyre size* 5.25 × 17 front, 7.00 × 22 rear *Height* 3 ft 5 ins *Weight* 16¼ cwt (unladen) *Average speed* 190 m.p.h. max. (approx.)

FORD POPULAR 1933

This was the first Ford to be designed in Britain for the British market. Instead of the large engine popular in the U.S., a small economy engine was fitted. Cheap to buy and cheap to run, it quickly became a popular car.

CHASSIS *Suspension (front)* $\frac{1}{2}$ elliptic *(rear)* $\frac{1}{2}$ elliptic *Brakes* 4 wheel

ENGINE *Tank capacity* $6\frac{1}{2}$ galls. *No. of Cyls.* 4 *Carburettors* 1 *Max. B.H.P.* 8 (rated) *Capacity* 933 c.c. *Ignition* Coil

DOORS 4

TRANSMISSION *Clutch* disk *Gearbox* 3 speed and reverse *Final Drive* Shaft

DIMENSIONS, ETC.

Four seater *Length* 11 ft 11 ins *Width* 4 ft 6 ins *Wheelbase* 7 ft 6 ins *Tyre size* 4.50 × 17 *Height* 5 ft 4 ins *Weight* 13 cwt *Average speed* 58 m.p.h. max.

The 7 cv was quite revolutionary. It had a metal hull without the customary chassis underneath, and front wheel drive, which up until then, had not been used on a mass-produced car. The Citroen quickly became a firm favourite. Components from this design were the basis of several other makes of car, such as the George Irat and the later Rosengart. This series of car was in production until 1957. About 700,000 were made.

CHASSIS *Suspension (front)* Independent, torsion bars *(rear)* Torsion bars *Brakes* 4 wheel brakes, hydraulic
ENGINE *No. of Cyls.* 4 *Carburettors* 1 Solex *Capacity* 1,303 c.c. *Ignition* Coil
DOORS 4
TRANSMISSION *Clutch* Single disk *Gearbox* 4 speeds and reverse *Final Drive* Shaft
DIMENSIONS, ETC. Saloon *Length* 14 ft $8\frac{3}{4}$ ins *Width* 5 ft $3\frac{1}{2}$ ins *Wheelbase* 9 ft 6 ins *Height* 4 ft $8\frac{1}{2}$ ins *Weight* 18 cwt *Average speed* 68 m.p.h. max.

CHRYSLER AIRFLOW 1934

The Chrysler 'Airflow' was the first car with an aerodynamic body to be put into large-scale production. Its performance was good for the time, and the lower degree of 'wind noise' made it a pleasure to travel in. It was not a commercial success however and production ceased after about 2 years.

CHASSIS *Suspension (front)* $\frac{1}{2}$ elliptic *(rear)* $\frac{1}{2}$ elliptic *Brakes* Hydraulic 4 wheel brakes
ENGINE *No. of Cyls.* 6 *Carburettors* 1 *Ignition* Coil
DOORS 4
TRANSMISSION *Clutch* Single plate *Gearbox* 3 speed and reverse (Syncromesh) *Final Drive* Shaft to bevel gear
DIMENSIONS, ETC.
Four—six seater *Length* 15 ft 1$\frac{1}{2}$ ins

**FRAZER NASH
TYPE 2
1934**

The Frazer Nash was one of the two most popular British sports cars of the inter-war period (the other being the Aston-Martin). Its sv water-cooled 4-cylinder, 1½ litre Anzani engine was later replaced by a Meadows engine with overhead valves.

CHASSIS *Suspension (front)* ¼ elliptic *(rear)* ¼ elliptic *Brakes* 4 wheel brakes
ENGINE *Tank capacity* 13 galls. *No. of Cyls.* 6 *Capacity* 1,498 c.c. *Ignition* Coil
DOORS 1 or none
TRANSMISSION *Gearbox* 4 speeds and reverse *Final Drive* Chains
DIMENSIONS, ETC.
Two–three seater *Length* 11 ft 11 ins *Width* 3 ft 4 ins *Wheelbase* 9 ft *Tyre size* 27 × 4.40 *Height* 4 ft *Weight* 18 cwt *Average speed* Cruising 60/70. Max. 87

CHEVROLET STANDARD SALOON 1935

This car is typical of the big family car popular in America. It was reliable and gave good service for a long time. The Chevrolet Standard was more comfortable than the average European family car.

CHASSIS *Suspension (front)* Semi-elliptic *(rear)* Semi-elliptic *Brakes* 4 wheel brakes. Hydraulic

ENGINE *Tank capacity* 11 galls. *No. of Cyls.* 6 *Carburettors* 1 *Max. B.H.P.* 74 *Ignition* Coil

DOORS 4

TRANSMISSION *Clutch* Single dry plate *Gearbox* 3 speed and reverse. Synchromesh *Final Drive* Shaft to bevel

DIMENSIONS, ETC. Five seater *Length* 15 ft 5 ins *Width* 5 ft 6 ins *Wheelbase* 8 ft 11 ins *Height* 5 ft 6 ins *Weight* 24 cwt *Average speed* 68 m.p.h. max.

The first sports car of S.S. Cars (now Jaguar Cars Ltd.), appeared in 1935. It had a short chassis and two-seater bodywork. Although now a collector's piece, in its day, the S.S. 100 was not over-popular with sports car drivers. Nowadays, a good S.S. 100 fetches a high price.

S.S. (JAGUAR) 2½ LITRE SPORTS 1935

CHASSIS *Suspension (front)* Semi-elliptic *(rear)* Semi-elliptic *Brakes* Girling—rod-operated

ENGINE *Tank capacity* 14 galls. *No. of Cyls.* 6 *Carburettors* 2 S.U. *Max. B.H.P.* 125 *Capacity* 3,485 c.c. *Ignition* Coil

DOORS 2

TRANSMISSION *Clutch* Single dry plate *Gearbox* 4-speed synchromesh *Final Drive* Spiral-bevel

STEERING Burman-Douglas, worm and nut

DIMENSIONS, ETC. Two seater *Length* 12 ft 9 ins *Width* 5 ft 2 ins *Wheelbase* 8 ft 8 ins *Height* 4 ft 7 ins with hood up *Weight* 23 cwt *Maximum speed* 95 m.p.h.

AUSTIN RACER 1936

This was the last of the Austin 750 c.c. racing cars. It had a new-type cooling system. Austin Seven-based sports and racing cars had an almost unbelievable record of success before the Second World War. After the war, the sports cars were still used but eventually the Austin became a hill climb and 'special' car.

CHASSIS *Suspension (front)* Transverse spring *(rear)* $\frac{1}{4}$ elliptic *Brakes* Cable operated 12 ins drum F, 10 ins drum R

ENGINE Designed to run normally up to 9,400 r.p.m. *No. of Cyls.* 4 *Carburettors* SU *Max. B.H.P.* 116 *Capacity* 750 c.c. *Ignition* Coil

TRANSMISSION *Clutch* Disk *Gearbox* 5.5:1 top gear *Final Drive* Double reduction

DIMENSIONS, ETC. *Length* 10 ft *Width* 4 ft 6 ins *Wheelbase* 6 ft 10 ins *Height* 3 ft 6 ins *Weight* $9\frac{3}{4}$ cwt

The B.M.W. firm in Germany started by making Austin Sevens under licence, from which they progressed to an exciting range of home-designed cars, including the 326 Saloon and the 328 Sports two seater. The 328 was making quite a name for itself in the competition world when the war put a finish to its career.

CHASSIS *Suspension (rear)* $\frac{1}{2}$ elliptic *Brakes* 4 wheel brakes
ENGINE *No. of Cyls.* 6 *Carburettors* 2 *Max. B.H.P.* 50 *Capacity* 1,971 c.c. *Ignition* Coil
DOORS 4
TRANSMISSION *Clutch* Disk *Gearbox* 4 speed and reverse, syncromesh *Final Drive* Shaft to bevel gear
DIMENSIONS, ETC.
Four seater *Length* 15 ft 2$\frac{1}{2}$ ins *Width* 5 ft 2$\frac{3}{4}$ ins *Wheelbase* 9 ft 7$\frac{1}{2}$ ins *Height* 5 ft 4$\frac{3}{4}$ ins *Weight* 20 cwt *Average speed* 80 m.p.h. max.

FIAT
500 SALOON
1936–48

The Fiat 500 was originally designed in 1915 but production was not started until 1936 with a rather pleasant, simple bodywork, and a canvas roof. It was immensely popular and sold in huge numbers all over Europe where it could be seen as a town car or farmer's hack. This car probably set the fashion for mini-cars, and its tiny engine gave a fantastic fuel consumption—somewhere around 50–55 miles to the gallon.

CHASSIS *Suspension (front)* $\frac{1}{2}$ elliptic *(rear)* $\frac{1}{2}$ elliptic *Brakes* 4 wheel brakes, hydraulic

ENGINE *No. of Cyls.* 4 *Carburettors* 1 *Max. B.H.P.* 13 *Capacity* 569 c.c. *Ignition* Coil

DOORS 2

TRANSMISSION *Clutch* Multi-disk *Gearbox* 4 speed and reverse, synchromesh *Final Drive* Shaft to bevel gear

DIMENSIONS, ETC.
Two seater *Length* 10 ft 8$\frac{1}{2}$ ins *Width* 4 ft 3 ins *Wheelbase* 6 ft 6 ins *Tyre size* 4.00 × 15 *Height* 5 ft 6 ins *Weight* 7 cwt *Average speed* 60 m.p.h. max.

Last of the pre-war models, 'Phantom III' is considered one of the best-built cars ever. It had various types of doors and seating. Nowadays it would be extremely expensive to build. The chassis alone would cost about £20,000.

CHASSIS *Suspension (front)* I.F.S. front *(rear)* Semi-elliptic *Brakes* Internal expanding front, and rear mechanical servo

ENGINE *Tank capacity* 33 galls. *No. of Cyls.* 12 in V *Carburettors* 1 *Max. B.H.P.* 50.7 R.A.C. rating *Capacity* 7,340 c.c.

TRANSMISSION Clutch Single dry plate *Gearbox* 4 speed synchromesh, 1 reverse *Final Drive* Hypoid bevel

STEERING Marlas cam and roller

DIMENSIONS, ETC. *Length* 191 ins *Width* 77 ins *Wheelbase* 142 ins *Ground clearance* $7\frac{1}{2}$ ins *Height* Various *Weight* Chassis only 4,050 lb *Average speed* 100 m.p.h.

VAUXHALL "25" SALOON 1936

This car is one of the larger cars built by Vauxhall in the thirties, when they produced a wider range, rather than we see today. It was probably a mixture of American and British ideas. Somehow the big Vauxhalls were not too well received but the smaller cars sold well.

CHASSIS *Suspension (front)* Independent, torsion bars and coil springs *(rear)* $\frac{1}{2}$ elliptic and torsion bars *Brakes* 4 wheel brakes, hydraulic
ENGINE *Tank capacity* 12 galls. *No. of Cyls.* 6 *Carburettors* 1 Zenith *Max B.H.P.* 80 *Capacity* 3,215 c.c. *Ignition* Coil
TRANSMISSION *Clutch* Disk *Gearbox* 3 speeds and reverse, synchromesh *Final Drive* Shaft to bevel gear
DIMENSIONS, ETC.
Six seater *Length* 15 ft $4\frac{1}{4}$ ins *Width* 5 ft $11\frac{1}{2}$ ins *Wheelbase* 9 ft 3 ins *Tyre size* 6.25 × 16.

VOLKSWAGEN TYPE "60" SALOON 1936

Although this was the prototype for the Volkswagen as we know it today, it was never put into production in large numbers before the War. During the War various versions were built for the German forces, the Kubelwagen and the Schwimmwagen being the best known. After the war, a new factory was built at Wolfsburg and the car was put into mass production. The result was a success story to rival that of the Model 'T' Ford.

CHASSIS *Brakes* 4 wheel
ENGINE *No. of Cyls.* 4 *Carburettors* 1 Solex *Max. B.H.P.* 22 *Capacity* 984 c.c. *Ignition* Coil
TRANSMISSION *Clutch* disk *Gearbox* 4 speeds and reverse (synchromesh)
DIMENSIONS, ETC.
Four seater *Length* 12 ft 9 ins *Width* 4 ft 11 ins *Wheelbase* 7 ft 9¾ ins *Tyre size* 4.50 × 17 *Height* 4 ft 11 ins *Weight* 12 cwt approx *Average speed* 72 m.p.h. max. approx.

MORRIS
25 COUPE SALOON
1937

Morris's largest model sold for £320. The pre-war Wolseley cars built by the Morris factory, were well made and very comfortable. The version shown had a sports saloon body with a sunshine roof, typical of British cars of the period.

CHASSIS *Suspension* Semi-elliptic leaf springs *(front and rear) Brakes* Hydraulic on 4 wheels

ENGINE *Tank capacity* 13 galls *No. of Cyls.* 6 *Carburettors* SU *Max. B.H.P.* 79 at 3,700 *Capacity* 3,485 c.c. *Ignition* Coil

DOORS 4

TRANSMISSION *Clutch* Single dry plate *Gearbox* 3 speeds and reverse, synchromesh *Final Drive* Spiral bevel

DIMENSIONS, ETC.

Four-five seater *Length* 15 ft 8 ins *Width* 5 ft 10 ins *Wheelbase* 10 ft $1\frac{1}{2}$ ins *Tyre size* 600 × 17 *Height* 5 ft 9 ins *Weight* $29\frac{3}{4}$ cwt *Test speed* 77.59 m.p.h. *Cruising speed* 65 m.p.h.

All Maybach cars were 'handmade'. Output was low but the quality superb. Up to seven passengers could be carried, including the chauffeur. They were popular amongst the Nazi hierarchy, and many of the superb cars to be seen on films of parades in Nazi Germany were made by Maybach. (The other two popular makes were Horsch and Mercedes-Benz.)

CHASSIS *Suspension (rear)* Leaf springs *Brakes* Mechanical 4 wheel brake
ENGINE *Name* Maybach model HL.38 *No. of Cyls.* 6 *Carburettors* Solex Special *Max. B.H.P.* 140 b.h.p. at 4,000 r.p.m. *Capacity* 3,800 c.c. *Ignition* Coil
DOORS 4
TRANSMISSION *Gearbox* Maybach five speeds forward; 1 speed backward
DIMENSIONS, ETC.
Seven seater *Length* 16 ft 6 ins *Width* 6 ft 1 ins *Wheelbase* 11 ft 1 in and 12 ft 1 in *Tyre size* 6.50 × 17 *Height* 5 ft 6 ins *Weight* 4,000 to 4,800 lb according to body type (cabriolet or limousine)

MORRIS
8 SERIES E SALOON
1939

The Morris 8 series E was a continuation of the Morris 8 series started in the early thirties and built as a cheap family car, cheap to buy and to run. It was popular and sold well and was continued for a short period after the war. It was also used as a van by the Post Office.

CHASSIS *Suspension (front)* $\frac{1}{2}$ elliptic *(rear)* $\frac{1}{2}$ elliptic *Brakes* 4 wheel, hydraulic
ENGINE *Tank capacity* $5\frac{1}{2}$ galls. *No. of Cyls.* 4 *Carburettors* 1 S.U. *Max. B.H.P.* 29.5 *Capacity* 918 c.c.
DOORS 4
TRANSMISSION *Clutch* Single dry plate *Gearbox* 4 speed and reverse, synchromesh *Final Drive* Shaft to bevel gear
DIMENSIONS, ETC.
Four seater *Length* 12 ft *Width* 4 ft 9 ins *Wheelbase* 7 ft 5 ins *Tyre size* 4.50 × 17 *Height* 5 ft 2 ins *Weight* $15\frac{1}{4}$ cwt *Average speed* 56 m.p.h. (max).

WOLSELEY TEN SALOON 1939

The nicely-built pre-war Wolseley was something of a cheap luxury car. It was much better fitted out than one would expect. Lord Nuffield drove one of these cars for many years. Wolseley became just another B.M.C. car with a different radiator after the war.

CHASSIS *Suspension (front)* Leaf springs *(rear)* Leaf springs *Brakes* Hydraulic drum 9 ins dia.

ENGINE *Tank capacity* 7 galls. *No. of Cyls.* 4 *Carburettors* SU *Max. B.H.P.* 40 at 4,400 *Capacity* 1.140 c.c.

DOORS 4

TRANSMISSION *Clutch* Borg & Beck 8 ins single dry plate *Gearbox* 4 speed and reverse, synchromesh *Final Drive* Shaft to bevel gear

STEERING Bishop cam and lever

DIMENSIONS, ETC. Four seater *Length* 12 ft 3 ins *Width* 4 ft 9 ins *Wheelbase* 7 ft 6 ins *Ground clearance* 6½ ins *Height* 5 ft 1¼ ins *Weight* 19 cwt *Average speed* 65 m.p.h. approx.

RILEY
2½ LITRE
1946/53

A high performance Sports saloon with attractive lines. These cars gave excellent service and had long life. They are nowadays referred to as 'the last proper Rileys' because after this, Riley cars were just a different badge on a B.M.C. car. A Riley of this type in good condition is now a collector's piece.

CHASSIS *Suspension (front)* Torsion bar *(rear)* Semi-elliptic springs *Brakes* Girling Hydro mechanical. Later, full hydraulic

ENGINE *Name* Riley *Tank capacity* 12½ galls. *No. of Cyls.* 4 *Carburettors* 2 SU *Max. B.H.P.* 92, later increased to 100 *Capacity* 2,242 c.c. *Ignition* Coil

DOORS 4 (2 on Drophead)

TRANSMISSION *Clutch* Single plate *Gearbox* 4 speed, synchromesh *Final Drive* Torque tube to spiral bevel

STEERING Rack and pinion

DIMENSIONS, ETC.
Four seater *Length* 15 ft 5½ ins *Width* 5 ft 3½ ins. *Wheelbase* 9 ft 11 ins *Ground clearance* 7 ins *Height* 4 ft 11 ins *Weight* 28¾ cwt *Average speed* Max. 90 m.p.h. Later 95 m.p.h.

These cars, with bodywork largely made of aluminium, were rather a throwback to the thirties, when the razor-edged saloon was popular on Bentleys and Rolls-Royce cars. The Triumph enjoyed solid popularity though it was considered rather 'Aunty'. Many of these cars have survived in good condition and will become collector's cars in a few years. Later versions of the car were fitted with the 2 litre Standard Vanguard engine which improved the performance.

CHASSIS *Suspension (front)* Independent, transverse leaf *(rear)* Semi-elliptic leaf springs *Brakes* Drum—front and rear hydraulic
ENGINE *Tank capacity* 10 galls *No. of Cyls.* 4 *Carburettors* 1 Solex *Max. B.H.P.* $62\frac{1}{2}$ at 4,400 r.p.m. *Capacity* 1,776 c.c. *Ignition* Coil
TRANSMISSION *Clutch* Single dry plate *Gearbox* 4 speed, column change, synchromesh 2nd, 3rd and top *Final Drive* Hypoid, 4.86:1
DIMENSIONS, ETC. Six seater *Length* 14 ft 7 ins *Width* 5 ft 4 ins *Wheelbase* 9 ft *Ground clearance* 7 ins *Height* 5 ft 3 ins *Weight* 25-1-0 cwt *Top speed* 65 m.p.h.

BRISTOL
400 2 LITRE COUPE
SALOON 1947

When the Bristol 400 was introduced it caused quite a stir in motoring circles. Here was a good-looking car with performance and seats for four that was modern and attractive. The body design had a touch of the pre-war B.M.W. about it but for all that it was a modern design. The car was developed, and a series of cars have been built down to the present day. Nowadays an early Bristol can sometimes be bought fairly cheaply and it would be a very good car to buy.

CHASSIS *Suspension (front)* Independent—Transverse leaf spring *(rear)* 'Live' axle—Torsion bars *Brakes* Lockheed hydraulic—drum

ENGINE *Tank capacity* 12 galls. *No. of Cyls.* 6 *Carburettors* 3 Downdraught S.U. D.2 *Max. B.H.P.* 80 at 4,200 *Capacity* 1,971 c.c.

TRANSMISSION *Clutch* 8 ins single dry plate *Gearbox* Manual—4 forward, 1 reverse synchromesh 4th, 3rd & 2nd Freewheel 1st *Final Drive* Spiral bevel

DIMENSIONS, ETC.
Four seater *Length* 15 ft 3 ins *Width* 5 ft 4 ins *Wheelbase* 9 ft 6 ins *Ground clearance* 7 ins *Height* 4 ft 11 ins *Weight* 2,580 lb dry *Average speed* 95 m.p.h. max. approx.

This model, known in Britain as Renault 760 and 750, was really the first post-war mini-car. A very large number were sold.

RENAULT QUATRE CHEVAUX SALOON 1947

CHASSIS *Suspension (front and rear)* Coil spring all independent *Brakes* Hydraulic
ENGINE *Tank capacity* 6 galls. *No. of Cyls.* 4 *Carburettors* Solex *Max. B.H.P.* 19 at 4,000 *Capacity* 760 c.c. —1947 750 c.c.—1951 *Ignition* Coil
DOORS 4
TRANSMISSION *Clutch* Single dry plate *Gearbox* 3 speed *Final Drive* Spiral bevel
STEERING Rack and pinion
DIMENSIONS, ETC.
Four seater *Length* 11 ft 9½ ins *Width* 4 ft 8½ ins *Wheelbase* 6 ft 10½ ins *Ground clearance* 7⅛ ins *Height* 4 ft 10 ins *Weight* approx. 1,393 lb *Average speed* 65 m.p.h. approx. (max.)

STANDARD "VANGUARD" 1947

The Vanguard was the first new design to be produced by the Standard works after the war. The phase 1 was a very solid saloon car with some appeal and can still be seen on the road. Later cars did not have the sloping back—what we might call a 'fast back' today—they had a more conventional boot and somehow lost appeal. The engine was put into the T.R.2 after the Standard Triumph first became one vast group.

CHASSIS *Suspension (front)* Independent—double wishbone/coil springs *(rear)* Rigid axle—$\frac{1}{2}$ elliptic leaf springs *Brakes* Drum front and rear

ENGINE *Tank capacity* 15 galls. *No. of Cyls.* 4 *Carburettors* 1 Solex *Max. B.H.P.* 68 at 4,200 r.p.m. *Capacity* 2,088 c.c. *Ignition* Coil

TRANSMISSION *Clutch* Single dry plate *Gearbox* 3 speed, all-synchromesh, column change *Final Drive* Shaft to hypoid gear

STEERING Cam and peg

DIMENSIONS, ETC. Six seater *Length* 13 ft 10 ins *Width* 5 ft 9 ins *Wheelbase* 7 ft 10 ins *Tyre size* 5.90 × 15 *Height* 5 ft 4 ins *Weight* 25 cwt *Average speed* 75–80 m.p.h. maximum

This, the first post-war Rolls-Royce, continued in production with many refinements until 1955, when superseded by Silver Cloud. It had various types of doors and seating.

ROLLS ROYCE SILVER WRAITH 1947

CHASSIS *Suspension (front)* I.F.S. *(rear)* Semi-elliptic, leaf *Brakes* Mechanical servo, hydraulic front mechanical
ENGINE *Tank capacity* 18 galls. *No. of Cyls.* 6 *Carburettors* 1 *Max. B.H.P.* not revealed *Capacity* 4,257 c.c. *Ignition* Coil
TRANSMISSION *Clutch* Single dry plate *Gearbox* Manual 4 forward, 1 reverse *Final Drive* Hypoid spiral
STEERING Cam and roller
DIMENSIONS, ETC.
Length 200 ins *Width* 75 ins *Wheelbase* 127 ins *Height* Various *Weight* Approx. 2 tons depending on body type *Average speed* 90 m.p.h.

JAGUAR XK 120 SPORTS 1948

When in 1948 Jaguar introduced the XK120 it achieved instant popularity, the performance in those days being quite astonishing for a production car of moderate price. Developments of the original design were used for record breaking and racing, and the successes of the 'C' types at Le Mans were similar in many ways to the fabulous successes of the Bentley Boys in the late twenties. Since then the type has been developed into the XK150, the 'D' type sports racing car and the current 'E' type.

CHASSIS *Suspension (front)* Independent (wishbone and torsion bars) *(rear)* Semi-elliptic *Brakes* Lockheed 2L5 hydraulic

ENGINE *Tank capacity* 14 galls. *No. of Cyls.* 6 *Carburettors* 2 SU *Max. B.H.P.* 160 at 5,000 r.p.m. *Capacity* 3,442 c.c. *Ignition* Coil

TRANSMISSION *Clutch* SDP *Gearbox* 4 spd synchro. *Final Drive* Hypoid bevel

STEERING Burman recirculating ball

DIMENSIONS, ETC.
Two seater *Length* 14 ft 5 ins *Width* 5 ft $1\frac{1}{2}$ ins *Wheelbase* 8 ft 6 ins *Height* 4 ft $4\frac{1}{2}$ ins (hood up) *Weight* 24 cwt *Max speed* 125 m.p.h.

MORRIS SIX SALOON 1948

This car is a typical family car of the late forties and early fifties. The body design bears obvious similarities to the Morris 'Minor', especially from the windscreen back. This car saw the introduction of 'badge engineering' for, with a different radiator grill and a few extra luxuries inside, the car became a Wolseley!

CHASSIS *Suspension (front)* Independent torsion bars and wishbones *(rear)* $\frac{1}{2}$ elliptic *Brakes* Lockheed hyd. 10 ins dia.

ENGINE *Tank capacity* 12 galls *No. of Cyls.* 6 *Carburettors* SU *Max. B.H.P.* 72.3 at 4,600 *Capacity* 2,214 c.c. *Ignition* Coil

DOORS 4

TRANSMISSION *Clutch* Single dry plate *Gearbox* 4 speed and reverse, synchromesh *Final Drive* Hypoid bevel

STEERING Bishop cam and roller

DIMENSIONS, ETC.

Four–five seater *Length* 14 ft 9 ins *Width* 5 ft 6 ins *Wheelbase* 9 ft 2 ins *Tyre size* 650 × 15 *Height* 5 ft 3$\frac{1}{2}$ ins *Weight* 24$\frac{1}{4}$ cwt *Average speed* 80 m.p.h. max.

PEUGEOT BERLINE 203 SALOON 1948

The Peugeot 203 was a popular car in France, being *the* car for respectable middle-class families to own. While it was technically not exciting, the performance achieved was better than one would expect from such a small engine in a large body. But the car went well, and sold well, and from it a whole family of cars has developed down to today when thousands of French families have a Peugeot.

CHASSIS *Suspension (front)* I.F.S. *(rear)* $\frac{1}{2}$ elliptic *Brakes* Hydraulic 4 wheels

ENGINE *No. of Cyls.* 4 *Carburettors* 1 *Max. B.H.P.* 49 *Capacity* 1,290 c.c. *Ignition* Coil

DOORS 4

TRANSMISSION *Gearbox* 4 speed and reverse. Synchromesh.

DIMENSIONS, ETC. Four seater *Length* 14 ft 7 ins *Width* 5 ft 3$\frac{1}{2}$ ins *Weight* 17 cwt approx.

The Morris Minor was introduced in 1949 and was then just another small car. Since then, well over a million have been sold and the car has been improved in detail, although basically it is still very much the same car. At one time, after the Austin-Morris merger the Minor was fitted with the smaller Austin A.30 engine, but this was not so popular and the present 1000 range have a new engine. The car is still with us, cheerful and timeless.

CHASSIS *Suspension (front)* Independent, torsion bars and wishbones *(rear)* Semi-elliptic leaf springs *Brakes* Lockheed hydraulic drums
ENGINE *Tank capacity* 5 galls. *No. of Cyls.* 4 *Carburettors* SU *Max. B.H.P.* 27.6 at 4,400 *Capacity* 918 c.c. *Ignition* Coil
DOORS 2
TRANSMISSION *Clutch* Borg & Beck $6\frac{1}{4}$ ins single dry plate *Gearbox* 4 speed and reverse, synchromesh *Final Drive* Semi-floating hypoid bevel
STEERING Rack and pinion
DIMENSIONS, ETC.
Four seater *Length* 12 ft 4 ins *Width* 5 ft 1 in *Wheelbase* 7 ft 2 ins *Tyre size* 500 × 14 *Height* 5 ft *Weight* $16\frac{3}{4}$ cwt *Average speed* 72 m.p.h.

M.G.
MIDGET T.D. SPORTS
1950

The T.D. was the first new Sports car to come from M.G. after the War, as the T.C. had been in production before the War. Both types were immensely popular and sold in large numbers both in Britain and America. The T.D. was really only a refinement of the T.C. Disk wheels replaced the not much lighter and more expensive wire wheels. Bumpers became standard.

CHASSIS *Suspension (front)* Independent, coil springs *(rear)* $\frac{1}{2}$ elliptic *Brakes* 4 wheel brakes, hydraulic
ENGINE *Tank capacity* $12\frac{1}{2}$ galls. *No. of Cyls.* 4 *Carburettors* 1 S.U. *Max. B.H.P.* 54 *Capacity* 1,250 c.c. *Ignition* Coil
DOORS 2
TRANSMISSION *Clutch* Single dry plate *Gearbox* 4 speeds and reverse, synchromesh *Final Drive* Shaft to hypoid bevel gear
DIMENSIONS, ETC.
Two seater *Length* 12 ft 1 in *Width* 4 ft 10 ins *Wheelbase* 7 ft 10 ins *Tyre size* 5.50 × 15 *Height* 4 ft 8 ins *Weight* $17\frac{3}{4}$ cwt *Average speed* 85 m.p.h. max. (approx.)

The Atlantic was an attempt by Austin to build a modern-looking car that was different. In this they succeeded, and the car was successful in world record attempts and in competition work. An open version was also made with a hood that folded away quite neatly, but the Atlantic was never a popular car and nowadays it is rare to see one on the road.

**AUSTIN
A90 ATLANTIC
SPORTS SALOON
1952**

CHASSIS *Suspension (front)* Independent. Coil springs *(rear)* Semi-elliptic *Brakes* Girling hydc. drums 11 ins **ENGINE** *Tank capacity* $12\frac{1}{2}$ galls. *No. of Cyls.* 4 *Carburettors* Twin SU *Max. B.H.P.* 88 at 4,000 *Capacity* 2,660 c.c. *Ignition* Coil **DOORS** 2 **TRANSMISSION** *Clutch* Single dry plate *Gearbox* 4 speed and reverse, synchromesh *Final Drive* Shaft to spiral bevel **STEERING** Cam and lever **DIMENSIONS, ETC.** Four seater *Length* 14 ft $9\frac{1}{8}$ ins *Width* 5 ft 10 ins *Wheelbase* 8 ft *Tyre size* 5.50 × 16 *Height* 5 ft 1 in *Weight* 27 cwt *Average speed* 90 m.p.h. approx.

LANCIA AURELIA G.T. SALOON 1952

The Aurelia is one of the long range of high performance sporting cars built since the earliest days of motoring by Lancia. This type was quite popular and there are still many Aurelias on the road.

CHASSIS *Suspension (front)* Independent with coil springs *(rear)* ½ elliptic *Brakes* hydraulic 4 wheel
ENGINE *Tank capacity* 16½ galls. *No. of Cyls.* 4 *Carburettors* 1 Weber *Max. B.H.P.* 115 approx. *Capacity* 2,451 c.c. *Ignition* Coil
DOORS 2
TRANSMISSION *Clutch* Single plate *Gearbox* 4 speeds and reverse, synchromesh *Final Drive* De Dion type
DIMENSIONS, ETC. Four seater *Length* 14 ft 4 ins *Width* 5 ft 1¼ ins *Wheelbase* 8 ft 8 ins *Tyre size* 165 × 400 *Weight* 22 cwt *Average speed* Max speed 112 m.p.h.

The Humber Hawk is one of a series of car built by Humber intended as large family or business cars. They are, on the whole, well-built cars which provide comfortable transport for up to 6 people. Like many British cars built after the war, the MK V Hawk is austere by modern standards, but it is a pleasant car to drive.

HUMBER
HAWK Mk V SALOON
1953

CHASSIS *Suspension (front)* Independent, coil springs *(rear)* ½ elliptic *Brakes* 4 wheel brakes, hydraulic
ENGINE *Tank capacity* 10 galls. *No. of Cyls.* 4 *Carburettors* 1 *Max. B.H.P.* 16 (rated) *Capacity* 2,267 c.c.
DOORS 4
TRANSMISSION *Clutch* Disk *Gearbox* 4 speed and reverse, synchromesh *Final Drive* Shaft to bevel gear
DIMENSIONS, ETC.
Six seater *Length* 15 ft 1 in *Width* 5 ft 10 ins *Wheelbase* 8 ft 9 ins *Tyre size* 640 × 15 *Height* 5 ft 4¾ ins *Weight* 26½ cwt

DAIMLER "CONQUEST" OPEN ROADSTER 1953

The Daimler 'Conquest', the 'Conquest' Roadster and the slightly later 'Century Conquest' cars were all built round the same chassis with suitable modifications. (A slightly cheaper Lanchester was really a utility version with a different radiator grill.) These are beautiful cars, well made, quiet with ample performance—luxury cars that are not expensive. They were continued until the firm was bought out by Jaguar Cars Ltd. in 1960.

CHASSIS *Suspension (front)* Independent (torsion bars and wishbones) *(rear)* Semi-elliptic springs *Brakes* Girling hydromechanical
ENGINE *Tank capacity* 15 galls. *No. of Cyls.* 6 *Carburettors* 2 SU *Max. B.H.P.* 100 b.h.p. at 4,400 r.p.m. *Capacity* 2,433 c.c. *Ignition* Coil
DOORS 2
TRANSMISSION *Clutch and gearbox* Daimler fluid flywheel coupled to epicyclic preselective gearbox *Final Drive* Hypoid bevel
DIMENSIONS, ETC.
Two seater *Length* 14 ft 10 ins *Width* 5 ft $5\frac{1}{2}$ ins *Wheelbase* 8 ft 8 ins *Ground clearance* $6\frac{1}{2}$ ins *Height* 4 ft 7 ins (hood up) *Weight* $25\frac{1}{2}$ cwt *Max. speed* 101 m.p.h.

ROVER "90" P4 SALOON 1954

This Rover is one of a family produced since the original 'Cyclops Eye' brought out in the late forties: the 75, the 90, the 100 and the 105. They are all similar, except for the size of engine. They are well built, luxurious cars, but not sports cars, and have been called 'the poor man's Rolls-Royce' with some reason.

CHASSIS Welded box section *Suspension (front)* Independent coil spring *(rear)* Semi-elliptic leaf springs *Brakes* (front) *Girling hydraulic two leading shoe* (rear) *Girling hydraulic/mechanical*
ENGINE *Tank capacity* $11\frac{1}{2}$ galls. *No. of Cyls.* 6 *Carburettors* 1 S.U. *Max. B.H.P.* 90 at 4,500 r.p.m. *Ignition* Coil
DOORS 4
TRANSMISSION *Clutch* Single, dry plate *Gearbox* 4 forward speed and reverse
STEERING Burman re-circulating ball worm and nut; variable ratio
DIMENSIONS, ETC.
Four-five seater *Length* $178\frac{1}{4}$ ins *Width* $65\frac{5}{8}$ ins *Wheelbase* 111 ins *Tyre size* 6.40 × 15 *Height* $63\frac{3}{4}$ ins *Weight* 3,175 lb *Top speed* 85 m.p.h.

CITROEN
2 c.v. SALOON
1955

The soft-topped Citroen 2 c.v. was introduced as a cheap-to-buy and cheap-to-run car for everyone. The result, although strictly utility, has been a car popular amongst many people, both in and out of France.

The production prototypes were built in 1939 but the war intervened. Testing of components continued throughout the war, so that when the car was launched in 1948 it had years of development behind it.

CHASSIS *Suspension (front and rear)* Independent with longitudinal coil springs *Brakes* Hydraulic with drums
ENGINE *Tank capacity* $4\frac{1}{2}$ galls. *No. of Cyls.* 2 *Carburettors* 1 Solex *Max. B.H.P. 13.5 Capacity* 425 c.c. *Ignition* Coil
DOORS 4
TRANSMISSION *Clutch* Single dry plate *Gearbox* 4 speed synchromesh and reverse *Final Drive* Front wheel drive, hypoid bevel
DIMENSIONS, ETC.
Four seater *Length* 12 ft $4\frac{3}{4}$ ins *Width* 4 ft $10\frac{1}{4}$ ins *Wheelbase* 7 ft $10\frac{1}{2}$ ins *Tyre size* 4.90 × 15 *Height* 5 ft 3 ins *Weight* $9\frac{3}{4}$ cwt (dry) *Average speed* 55 m.p.h. max.

Ever since Vauxhall was taken over by General Motors in the late twenties their cars have become more and more American in flavour, concentrating on family saloons. This policy has become more pronounced since the war. The Cresta is a good example of a Vauxhall of the period, slightly bulbous, with rather too much chromium ornamentation for many people's fancy. Even so, it provided transport for thousands of families at a reasonable price.

CHASSIS *Suspension (front)* Independent, coil spring *(rear)* Semi-elliptic *Brakes* 4 wheel hydraulic
ENGINE *Tank capacity* 11 galls. *No. of Cyls.* 6 *Carburettors* 1 *Max. B.H.P.* 67 *Capacity* 2,262 c.c. *Ignition* Coil
DOORS 4
TRANSMISSION *Clutch* Single disk *Gearbox* 3 speed and reverse, synchromesh *Final Drive* Shaft to hypoid bevel gear
DIMENSIONS, ETC.
Six seater *Length* 14 ft 4½ ins *Width* 5 ft 6½ ins *Wheelbase* 8 ft 7½ ins *Height* 5 ft 1½ ins *Weight* 22½ cwt *Average speed* 85 m.p.h. max.

VOLVO
PV 444 1.4 LITRE
SALOON 1955

The Volvo PV 444 established the general high reputation of Swedish cars that has continued with various models to this day. The Volvo and the Saab were built to drive in very arduous conditions, and so their successes in European Rallies have been many.

CHASSIS *Suspension (front)* I.F.S. coil springs *(rear)* Coil springs *Brakes* Hydraulic brakes, drum
ENGINE *Tank capacity* 7¾ galls. *No. of Cyls.* 4 *Carburettors* 1 Zenith *Max. B.H.P.* 75 *Capacity* 1,778 c.c. *Ignition* Coil
DOORS 2
TRANSMISSION *Clutch* Single plate *Gearbox* 4 speed and reverse *Final Drive* Hypoid bevel gear
DIMENSIONS, ETC.
Length: 14 ft 7 ins *Width* 5 ft 2½ ins *Wheelbase* 8 ft 6½ ins *Tyre size* 5.90 × 15 *Height* 5 ft 1½ ins *Weight* 19 cwt *Average speed* 93 m.p.h. max.

CITROEN
DS 19 SALOON
1956

When the DS 19 was introduced it was hailed as a great advance in design, but somehow it has not 'caught on'. Perhaps customers were suspicious of the complex suspension system, though it works well. Under the French taxation system, this is the largest car that it is worthwhile building, as, if the engine is any larger, the tax goes up and the car becomes expensive. The DS 19 is the car for the French professional man.

CHASSIS *Suspension (front and rear)* Independent with vacuum suspension and automatic levelling *Brakes* Hydraulic, disk front, drum rear
ENGINE *Tank capacity* 14¼ galls. *No. of Cyls.* 4 *Carburettors* 1 Solex *Max. B.H.P.* 70 *Capacity* 1,911 c.c. *Ignition* Coil
DOORS 4
TRANSMISSION *Clutch* Single dry plate *Gearbox* 4 speed synchromesh and reverse *Final Drive* Front wheel drive, spiral bevel
DIMENSIONS, ETC.
Five–six seater *Length* 15 ft 9 ins *Width* 5 ft 10¼ ins *Wheelbase* 10 ft 3 ins *Height* 4 ft 9¾ ins *Weight* 24 cwt *Average speed* 90 m.p.h. max.

RENAULT DAUPHINE SALOON 1956

The Dauphine was designed to be a popular-priced family car. Even today it is a very popular car. There are various versions available, including a Gordini version, rather like a Mini-Cooper.

CHASSIS *Suspension (front and rear)* Coil all independent *Brakes* Hydraulic 4 wheel

ENGINE *Tank capacity* 7 galls. *No. of Cyls.* 4 *Carburettors* Solex *Max. B.H.P.* 26.5 at 4,200 first *Capacity* 845 c.c. *Ignition* Coil

DOORS 4

TRANSMISSION *Clutch* Single dry plate *Gearbox* 3 speed (4 speed available 1960) and reverse *Final Drive* Spiral bevel

STEERING Rack and pinion

DIMENSIONS, ETC.
Four seater *Length* 12 ft 11 ins *Width* 5 ft *Wheelbase* 7 ft 5 ins *Tyre size* 5.50 × 15 *Height* 4 ft 9 ins *Weight* approx. 1,428 lb *Average speed* 72 m.p.h. max.

This car is really one of the last cars built to the old 'front-engined' school of thinking. Like many others it became outdated by the 1957 Cooper Climax. The Maserati Brothers have built racing cars and a few sports racing cars since the early twenties, and have enjoyed considerable success.

MASERATI 250 F FORMULA 1 GRAND PRIX 1957

CHASSIS *Suspension (front)* Independent, coil springs *(rear)* De Dion *Brakes* 4 wheel hydraulic (drums)
ENGINE *No. of Cyls* 6 *Carburettors* Weber *Max. B.H.P.* 270 *Capacity* 2,493 c.c.
TRANSMISSION *Clutch* Dry multidisk *Gearbox* 5 speeds and reverse *Final Drive* Shaft to bevel gears
DIMENSIONS, ETC.
Length 13 ft 5 ins *Width* 5 ft 4 ins *Wheelbase* 7 ft 5 ins *Tyre size* 5.50 × 16 *Height* 2 ft 10 ins *Weight* 11 cwt (dry) *Average speed* 185 m.p.h. max.

NSU
PRINZ SALOON
1958

The Prinz is sold as an economy car. Its performance and finish are both good. For two adults with two small children, it is a satisfactory little car.

CHASSIS *Suspension (front)* Independent with wishbones *(rear)* Independent with radius arms *Brakes* 4 wheel hydraulic
ENGINE *Tank capacity* 25 litres *No. of Cyls.* 2 *Carburettors* Downdraught Solex *Max. B.H.P.* 20 HP (DIN) at 4,600 r.p.m. *Capacity* 598 c.c. *Ignition* Coil
TRANSMISSION *Clutch* Dry single plate clutch, *Gearbox* 4 gears, 1 reverse, synchromesh *Final Drive* Hypoid bevel
STEERING Rack and pinion
DIMENSIONS, ETC.
Four seater *Length* 10 ft 4 ins *Width* 4 ft 8 ins *Wheelbase* 6 ft 7 ins *Height* 4 ft 5 ins *Weight* $9\frac{1}{2}$ cwt *Average speed* Top speed 68 m.p.h.

The DAF operated with two pedals without gearshift lever, the gearbox being entirely automatic. The DAF is better finished than many cheap cars and this has made this little car from Holland very popular.

CHASSIS *Suspension (front)* Transverse leaf springs *(rear)* Coil springs *Brakes* Hydraulic on all 4 wheels
ENGINE *Tank capacity* $6\frac{1}{4}$ galls. *No. of Cyls.* 2 *Carburettors* 1 *Max. B.H.P.* 22 (at 4,000 r.p.m.) *Capacity* 590 c.c. *Ignition* Coil
TRANSMISSION Continuous variable transmission and automatic reduction-selection
STEERING Rack and pinion
DIMENSIONS, ETC.
Four seater *Length* 142 ins *Width* 56 ins *Wheelbase* 81 ins *Tyre size* 4.10 × 14 *Height* 54 ins *Weight* (unladen) 1,323 lb *Maximum speed* 57 m.p.h.

SINGER GAZELLE SALOON 1959

The Gazelle is a de luxe version of the Rootes-built Hillman Minx. A different radiator and chromium trim was added, while inside the car the fittings are more luxurious and of better quality than those fitted to the Minx. An overdrive can be fitted if required.

CHASSIS *Suspension (front)* Independent—coil springs *(rear)* Semi-elliptic *Brakes* Lockheed hydraulic

ENGINE *Tank capacity* 10 galls. *Carburettors* 1 Solex 32 PBIS *Max. B.H.P.* 4:60 net at 4,600 r.p.m. *Capacity* 1,495 c.c. *Ignition* Coil

DOORS 4

TRANSMISSION *Clutch* Borg and Beck single dry plate *Gearbox* 4 speed, 1 reverse (synchromesh) *Final Drive* Semi-floating, spiral bevel

STEERING Burman 'F' type recirculating ball

DIMENSIONS, ETC. Four–five seater *Length* 163.5 ins *Width* 60.75 ins *Wheelbase* 96 ins *Tyre size* 5.60 × 15 *Height* 59.5 ins *Weight* (unladen) 2,316 lb *Average speed* 85–88 m.p.h. (max.)

The design by Alec Issigonis of the 'Mini' was a great step forward, in that a small car was built with ample room inside, while the front wheel drive and the unique suspension gave excellent road holding and the low weight gave good performance. The transverse position of the engine makes the bonnet much shorter than usual. This gives greater passenger space. The Mini will undoubtedly rank in history with the Model 'T', the 'Bullnose' Morris and the VW as a car for the millions.

BMC MINI SALOON 1959

CHASSIS *Suspension* Hydrolastic displacers inter-connected front and rear *Brakes* Lockheed hydraulic 7 ins drums

ENGINE *Tank capacity* $5\frac{1}{2}$ galls. *No. of Cyls.* 4 *Carburettors* SU *Max. B.H.P.* 34 at 5,500 *Capacity* 848 c.c. *Ignition* Coil

DOORS 2

TRANSMISSION *Clutch* Borg & Beck diaphragm spring *Gearbox* 4 speed and reverse, synchromesh

STEERING Rack and pinion

DIMENSIONS, ETC.
Four seater *Length* 10 ft $0\frac{1}{2}$ ins *Width* 4 ft $7\frac{1}{2}$ ins *Wheelbase* 6 ft $8\frac{1}{4}$ ins *Tyre size* 5.20 × 10 *Height* 4 ft 5 ins *Weight* 1,398 lb *Average speed* 72 m.p.h.

HJO 151

AUSTIN
A55 CAMBRIDGE
Mk II SALOON
1959–1961

This car differs from the MK 1 chiefly in the matter of chromium trim and the shape of the rear boot. The earlier model had a blunter rear end with less luggage space. These cars, if looked after, are thoroughly reliable and will continue to give good service for very many years. They are not sports cars and are intended as family saloons, the job that they do very well.

CHASSIS *Suspension (front)* Independent coil spring *(rear)* Semi-elliptic leaf spring *Brakes* Girling hydc.

ENGINE *Tank capacity* 10 galls. *Carburettors* SU *No. of Cyls.* 4 *Max. B.H.P.* 53 at 4,350 *Capacity* 1,489 c.c. *Ignition* Coil

DOORS 4

TRANSMISSION *Clutch* Borg & Beck 8 ins single dry plate *Gearbox* 4 speed and reverse, synchromesh *Final Drive* Hypoid

STEERING Cam and lever

DIMENSIONS, ETC.
Four seater *Length* 14 ft $10\frac{1}{8}$ ins *Width* 5 ft $3\frac{1}{2}$ ins *Wheelbase* 8 ft $3\frac{3}{16}$ ins *Tyre size* 590 × 13 *Height* 4 ft $11\frac{3}{4}$ ins *Weight* $21\frac{1}{4}$ cwt *Average speed* 80 m.p.h.

VOLKSWAGEN
1200 SALOON
1960

This is the modified version of the famous 'VW' with larger rear window, etc. that has slowly evolved from the previous design of Dr. Porsche. The alterations are all small and have been introduced at various times, when convenient, on the production line. The VW can be seen on the roads all over the world, where it has made a name for itself for finish and reliability.

CHASSIS *Suspension (front)* Independent Torsion bars, *(rear)* Independent suspension, Torsion bars *Brakes* 4 wheel, hydraulic

ENGINE *Tank capacity* 8.8 Imp. Gal. *No. of Cyls.* 4 *Carburettors* Solex *Max. B.H.P.* 34 b.h.p. at 3,600 r.p.m. 41.5 b.h.p. at 3,900 r.p.m. *Capacity* 1,192 c.c. *Ignition* Coil

TRANSMISSION *Clutch* Fichtel & Sachs KS 180 *Gearbox* Fully synchronised four-speed gearbox *Final Drive* Spiral bevel

DIMENSIONS, ETC. Four seater *Length* 13 ft 4 ins *Width* 5 ft 1 in *Wheelbase* 6.50 × 15 *Height* 4 ft 11 ins *Weight* (unladen) 760 lb *Max speed* 71 m.p.h.

JAGUAR "E" TYPE 1961

The 'E' type Jaguar, which was much admired when it was introduced, is a superb GT machine, not a sports car, although it is faster than most sports cars. It has become rather luxurious inside, which makes it heavier than it need be. Many 'E' types have been exported to the U.S.A.

CHASSIS *Suspension (front)* Independent coil springs *(rear)* Independent coil springs *Brakes* Disks all round, servo assisted.

ENGINE *Tank capacity* 14 galls. *No. of Cyls.* 6 *Carburettors* 3 SU *Max. B.H.P.* 265 *Capacity* 3,781 c.c. *Ignition* Coil

DOORS 2

TRANSMISSION *Clutch* Single dry plate *Gearbox* 4 speed and reverse. Synchromesh *Final Drive* Shaft to hypoid bevel, limited slip final drive fitted

STEERING Rack and pinion

DIMENSIONS, ETC.

Two seater *Length* 14 ft $7\frac{1}{4}$ ins *Width* 5 ft $5\frac{1}{4}$ ins *Wheelbase* 8 ft *Tyre size* 6.40 × 15 *Height* 4 ft *Weight* 23 cwt *Average speed* 150 m.p.h. (max.)

PONTIAC TEMPEST SEDAN 1961

This car is one of the slightly less popular American cars, in that it is not in the top few as far as sales are concerned. The Pontiac is a typical car of the sixties in America, although the engine, a V-4, is rather small for an American car, where $3\frac{1}{2}$ litres is a common size. (Some cars, such as the Buick and the Cadillac, have engines of $6\frac{1}{2}$ litres.) Another unusual feature is the fitting of a manual gearbox instead of the usual automatic.

CHASSIS *Suspension (front)* Ball joint independent *(rear)* Independent, coil springs *Brakes* Hydraulic, 4 wheel
ENGINE *Tank capacity* 16 galls. *No. of Cyls.* 4 In-Head *Carburettors* 1 Rochester *Max. B.H.P.* 110 (at 3,800 r.p.m.) *Capacity* 3,180 c.c. *Ignition* Coil
DOORS 4
TRANSMISSION *Clutch* Borg and Beck single dry plate *Gearbox* 3 speed Synchromesh and reverse *Final Drive* Hypoid bevel
STEERING Recirculating ball
DIMENSIONS, ETC.
Six seater *Length* 189.3 ins *Width* 72.2 ins *Wheelbase* 112 ins *Tyre size* 6.00 × 15 *Height* 52.5 ins *Weight* 2,800 lb *Average speed* 93 m.p.h. (max.)

PORSCHE FORMULA 1 1962

After designing Auto Union racers, Mercedes cars and the Volkswagen, Ferdinand Porsche began to produce his own cars in 1948. Since then, Porsche cars have won many road and track races and hill climbs. Our picture shows Dan Gurney in 1962.

CHASSIS *Suspension (front)* Independent Torsion bar *(rear)* Independent Torsion bar *Brakes* Disks
ENGINE *No. of Cyls.* 8 *Carburettors* 4 Weber *Capacity* 1,494 c.c. *Ignition* Coil
TRANSMISSION *Gearbox* 6 speed and reverse
DIMENSIONS, ETC.
Length 11 ft 10 ins *Width* 4 ft 6 ins approx. *Wheelbase* 7 ft 6 ins *Tyre size* 5.00 × 15 (front), 6.50 × 15 (rear) *Height* 2 ft 7½ ins *Weight* 5 cwt *Average speed* 180 m.p.h. plus (max.)

RILEY
4/68 SALOON
1962

The most De Luxe of the B.M.C. 'B' Series Farina range, carrying the familiar Riley Radiator, had a wooden instrument panel and door cappings, the instruments incorporating a rev. counter. This is a familiar 1½ litre B.M.C. Austin/Morris car with a different radiator grill and a more luxurious interior. In 1969 B.M.C. stopped building 'Riley' cars, as they had lost their appeal and sales were so poor. Conversely, pre-war and 1946–55 cars are still much in demand.

CHASSIS *Suspension (front)* Coil spring *(rear)* Semi-elliptic *Brakes* Girling hydraulic

ENGINE B.M.C. *Tank capacity* 10 galls. *No. of Cyls.* 4 *Carburettors* 2 SU *Max. B.H.P.* 68, later 72 *Capacity* 1,498 c.c., later 1,622 c.c. *Ignition* Coil

DOORS 4

TRANSMISSION *Clutch* Borg & Beck single plate *Gearbox* 4 speed, synchromesh or Borg Warner Automatic transmission *Final Drive* Open prop shaft

STEERING Cam and lever

DIMENSIONS, ETC.

Four–five seater *Length* 14 ft 10 ins *Width* 5 ft 3½ ins *Wheelbase* 5 ft 3¼ ins *Tyre size* 5.90 × 14 *Height* 4 ft 11¼ ins *Weight* 25¾ cwt *Average speed* Max 88 m.p.h.

CHRYSLER NEW YORKER 1963

This Chrysler shows the improvement in body design in America since the early fifties. The design is much cleaner and simpler, without the useless chromium ornamentation that was typical of American cars of about 10 years previous.

CHASSIS *Suspension (front)* Independent, torsion bars *(rear)* $\frac{1}{2}$ elliptic *Brakes* 4 wheel servo (drums)

ENGINE *Tank capacity* 19 galls. *No. of Cyls.* V8 *Carburettors* 1 Carter *Max. B.H.P.* 340 *Capacity* 6,752 c.c. *Ignition* Coil

DOORS 4

TRANSMISSION *Gearbox* Automatic 'Torquflite' 3 speeds and reverse *Final Drive* Shaft to hypoid bevel

DIMENSIONS, ETC.
Six seater *Length* 17 ft 11 ins *Width* 6 ft 7 ins *Wheelbase* 10 ft 2 ins *Tyre size* 8.50 × 14 *Height* 4 ft 7 ins *Weight* 36 cwt *Average speed* 115 m.p.h. speed

This Rootes Group car is a continuation of the Hillman 'Minx' series. The lines are simple and restrained, and the Minx has a good all-round reputation as a family saloon.

HILLMAN MINX DE LUXE 1600 1963

CHASSIS *Suspension (front)* Independent—coil springs *(rear)* Live axle—semi-elliptic *Brakes* Lockheed Hydraulic Disk
ENGINE *Tank capacity* 10 galls. *No. of Cyls.* 4 *Carburettors* Solex 33 PSE 1 *Max. B.H.P.* 4: 52.8 B.H.P. nett at 4,100 r.p.m. *Capacity* 1,592 c.c. *Ignition* Coil
DOORS 4
TRANSMISSION *Clutch* Borg and Beck, Single Dry Plate *Gearbox* 4 speed, 1 reverse, synchromesh *Final Drive* Semi-floating: Hypoid
STEERING Burman 'F' type Recirculating Ball
DIMENSIONS, ETC.
Four—five seater *Length* 161.5 ins *Width* 60.75 ins *Wheelbase* 96.0 ins *Tyre size* 600 × 13 *Height* 58.0 ins *Weight (unladen)* 19½ cwt *Average speed* 76–79 m.p.h.

MORRIS 1100 SALOON 1961–1964

The Morris 1100 is a bigger brother of the 'Mini-Minor', having the same mechanical layout of transverse engine with gearbox below driving the front wheels through Birfield jointed shafts with hydrolastic suspension. While the engine is larger in the 1100, the performance is only slightly improved, the extra power being used to propel the larger, heavier and more comfortable body. The 1100 is a comfortable 4 seater while the Mini is rather limited in its room for the rear-seat passengers.

CHASSIS *Suspension (front) (rear)* Hydrolastic displacers inter-connected *Brakes* Lockheed hydraulic front Disk rear Drum

ENGINE *Tank capacity* 8 galls. *No. of Cyls.* 4 *Carburettors* SU *Max. B.H.P.* 48 at 5,100 *Capacity* 1,098 c.c. *Ignition* Coil

DOORS 4

TRANSMISSION *Clutch* Diaphragm spring *Gearbox* 4 speed and reverse, synchromesh

STEERING Rack and pinion

DIMENSIONS, ETC.

Four seater *Length* 12 ft $2\frac{3}{4}$ ins *Width* 5 ft $0\frac{7}{8}$ ins *Wheelbase* 7 ft $9\frac{1}{2}$ ins *Tyre size* 5.50 × 12 *Height* 4 ft 5 ins *Weight* 1,834 lbs *Average speed* 77 m.p.h.

This G.T. car is built by Bond Ltd., and is based on components made by Triumph for the Herald series, with suitable modifications to improve the road holding and performance. The result is a high performance car that has a certain distinctive appeal that the mass-produced car often lacks. The Bond has the advantage that, much of the mechanical side being based on Triumph parts, there should not be a spares difficulty, which often applies to quite well known cars.

CHASSIS *Suspension (front)* Independent coil springs *(rear)* Independent *Brakes* Hydraulic, Disks front, Drums rear
ENGINE *Tank capacity* 10 galls. *No. of Cyls.* 4 *Carburettors* 2 *Max. B.H.P.* 75 *Capacity* 1,300 c.c. *Ignition* Coil
DOORS 2
TRANSMISSION *Clutch* Single plate (Hydraulic operation *Gearbox* 4 speed, synchromesh and reverse *Final Drive* Shaft to hypoid Bevel
DIMENSIONS, ETC.
Four seater *Length* 13 ft 1½ ins *Width* 5 ft *Wheelbase* 7 ft 7½ ins *Tyre size* 5.20 × 13 *Height* 4 ft 5 ins *Weight* 14½ cwt (Dry) *Average speed* 90 m.p.h. approx. max.

FERRARI OPEN SPORTS/ RACING 1965

This Sports/Racing car is one of a long line of Ferrari cars built since the war and entered with conspicuous success in most of the sporting events, both in America and in Europe. In this car the 4 litre engine is similar to the 400 Super-America Coupé built with the American market in mind, although the engine is mounted in the front on the latter model. Using this engine, the 400 Super-American Coupé has a top speed of 178 and a fuel consumption of 14 miles per gallon. All Ferraris are beautifully built and finished.

CHASSIS *Suspension (front)* Independent *(rear)* Independent *Brakes* Disks on 4 wheels **ENGINE** *No. of Cyls.* 12 V *Carburettors* 3 Weber *Max. B.H.P.* 340 plus *Capacity* 3,967 c.c. *Ignition* Coil **DOORS** 2 **TRANSMISSION** *Clutch* Single plate *Gearbox* Five speed and reverse **DIMENSIONS, ETC.** Two seater *Length* 13 ft $1\frac{1}{2}$ ins *Width* 4 ft $5\frac{3}{4}$ ins *Wheelbase* 8 ft 6 ins *Tyre size* 5.50 × 15 (front) 6.50 × 15 (rear) *Height* 3 ft 5 ins *Average speed* 180 m.p.h. plus (max.)

The Silver Shadow and the 'T' Series Bentley are the latest cars to come from Crewe. They are both superb cars, and are the first Rolls-Royce cars to have integral construction, abandoning the traditional chassis. These cars have almost every luxury built in, and, while some other cars may have a better performance or be better in some way or another, as a whole, these cars are still the best in the world.

CHASSIS *Suspension (front)* Independent coil spring *(rear)* Independent coil spring *Brakes* Disk

ENGINE *Tank capacity* 24 galls. *No. of Cyls.* 8 *Carburettors* 2 *Max. B.H.P.* Not revealed *Capacity* 6,230 c.c. *Ignition* Coil

DOORS 4

TRANSMISSION *Clutch and Gearbox* 3 speed automatic torque converter *Final Drive* Hypoid spiral

STEERING P.A.S. recirculating ball

DIMENSIONS, ETC.
Four—five seater *Length* 16 ft 11¾ ins *Width* 5 ft 11 ins. *Wheelbase* 10 ft 3 ins *Tyre size Height* 4 ft 11¾ ins *Weight* 41 cwt *Average speed* 110 plus m.p.h.

ROVER–B.R.M. GAS TURBINE ENTRY FOR 1965 LE MANS 1965

This car is one of a series built by Rover to test the practicability of the Gas Turbine engine for the motor-car. Built in conjunction with B.R.M., it did well at Le Mans, since when little has been heard of it. Experiments are continuing, and some day a practical gas turbine car will appear on the market.

CHASSIS *Suspension (front)* Unequal wishbones *(rear)* 4 link system as B.R.M. Formula 1 *Brakes* Twin Dunlop hydraulic discs

ENGINE *Name* Rover2S/150R 2 shaft regenerative gas turbine. Lucas 2 F.P. fuel pumps *Tank capacity* 24 galls. *Max. B.H.P.* 145

DOORS 2

TRANSMISSION *Clutch* none *Gearbox* Rubery Owen B.R.M. Type 57 single forward and reverse ratios

STEERING Rack and Pinion

DIMENSIONS, ETC.
Two seater *Length* 166½ ins *Width* 65½ ins *Wheelbase* 94½ ins *Ground clearance* 4½ ins *Height* 43⅝ ins *Weight* 1,580 lb dry *Average speed* 150 m.p.h. max.

This is a new 'fast back' version of the V.W. with a larger engine fitted. It has the usual V.W. reliability and good finish.

VOLKSWAGEN 1600 TL SALOON 1965

CHASSIS *Suspension (front)* Independent, torsion bars *(rear)* Independent, torsion bars *Brakes* Hydraulic, disks front, drums rear

ENGINE *Tank capacity* $8\frac{3}{4}$ galls. *No. of Cyls.* 4 *Carburettors* 1 Solex *Max. B.H.P.* 54 *Capacity* 1,584 c.c. *Ignition* Coil

DOORS 2

TRANSMISSION *Clutch* Dry disk *Gearbox* 4 speed synchromesh and reverse *Final Drive* Spiral bevel

STEERING Worm and roller

DIMENSIONS, ETC. Four seater *Length* 13 ft 10 ins *Width* 5 ft $4\frac{1}{2}$ ins *Wheelbase* 7 ft 10 ins *Tyre size* 6.00 × 15 *Height* 4 ft 9 ins *Weight* 19 cwt *Average speed* 78 m.p.h. max.

CHEVROLET CAPRICE SALOON 1966

The Chevrolet is a typically large, powerful American family car, built to stand rough heavy work in the country as well as shopping and driving to the station, in town. The Chevrolet is built in large numbers in various versions (Saloon, Convertible or Station Wagon), and the engineering that goes into these cars is superb.

CHASSIS *Suspension (rear)* Independent, coil springs *(rear)* Leaf springs *Brakes* Servo operated, Drum

ENGINE *Tank capacity* 20 galls. *No. of Cyls.* 8 *Carburettors* 1 *Max. B.H.P.* 195 *Capacity* 5351 c.c. *Ignition* Coil

DOORS 4

TRANSMISSION *Clutch* Single plate *Gearbox* 3 speed synchromesh and reverse *Final Drive* Hypoid bevel

STEERING Recirculating ball nut

DIMENSIONS, ETC.
Four–five seater *Length* 17 ft 9 ins *Width* 6 ft 7$\frac{1}{2}$ ins *Wheelbase* 9 ft 11 ins *Tyre size* 8.00 × 14 *Height* 4 ft 7$\frac{1}{2}$ ins *Weight*, 32 cwt *Average speed* 120 m.p.h. approx. (max.).

**FORD
ZODIAC Mk IV
SALOON
1966**

This new range—the Zephyr and Zodiac MK IV—is very different from the cars it replaced. The spare wheel goes in front of the engine, giving more luggage space, the V engine takes up less room, and safety has been built into the cars throughout. They give the impression of being much bigger than the previous range, although they are not much bigger in fact. They are comfortable, large cars and give a new image to Fords. An estate car version is also built, as is a larger 'executive' type car.

CHASSIS *Suspension (front)* Independent, coil springs *(rear)* Independent, coil springs *Brakes* Servo assisted disks

ENGINE *Tank capacity* 15 galls. *No. of Cyls.* V-6 *Carburettors* 1 *Max. B.H.P.* 118 *Capacity* 2,495 c.c. *Ignition* Coil

DOORS 4

TRANSMISSION *Clutch* Diaphragm spring clutch *Gearbox* 4 speed synchromesh and reverse *Final Drive* Shaft to hypoid bevel

DIMENSIONS, ETC.

Five–six seater *Length* 15 ft 5 ins *Width* 5 ft 11 ins *Wheelbase* 9 ft 7 ins *Tyre size* 6.40 × 13 *Height* 4 ft 8½ ins *Weight* 25 cwt *Average speed* 102.5 m.p.h. max.

JENSEN
FF SALOON
1966

The Jensen FF is the world's first and only production car to feature 4 wheel drive and Maxaret anti-lock braking. Despite the high price the Jensen has become popular, and it is surprising how many you see on the road. It is an advanced, well designed and beautifully-made car, and it is to be hoped that its safety features will eventually be incorporated in more mass-produced cars.

CHASSIS *Suspension (front)* Independent *Brakes* Girling 4 wheel disc with Maxaret anti-lock feature

ENGINE *No. of Cyls.* V8 *Carburettors* 1 *Max. B.H.P.* 325 *Capacity* 3,276 c.c. *Ignition* Coil

TRANSMISSION *Clutch/ Gearbox/Final Drive* Automatic transmission with 3 speeds and torque convertor coupled with Ferguson formula 4 wheel drive unit

STEERING Power assisted Rack and Pinion

DIMENSIONS, ETC.
Four seater *Length* 15 ft 11 ins *Width* 5 ft 9 ins *Wheelbase* 9 ft 1 ins *Ground clearance* $5\frac{3}{4}$ ins *Height* 4 ft 5 ins *Weight* 36 cwt *Average speed* 133 m.p.h. max.

This is another of the Ferrari racing/sports cars that have made Ferrari such a famous name in racing. The rear engine follows the Cooper design for a Formula I car. Most high performance cars for competition work, to be used at Le Mans and similar events, are now built to this design—rear engine low and with huge tyres for road holding. The sports car is becoming a specialized type, far from the usual family car.

FERRARI P4 SPORTS/RACING 1967

CHASSIS *Suspension (front/rear)* Independent 4-wheel
ENGINE Rear *Max B.H.P.* 450 *Ignition* Coil *No. of Cyls.* 12
DOORS 2
TRANSMISSION *Clutch Gearbox* 5 speed and reverse (Synchromesh)
DIMENSIONS, ETC.
Two seater *Length* 13 ft 7 ins *Width* 4 ft 7 ins *Wheelbase* 7 ft 9 ins *Tyre size* Front 10.15 × 15. Rear 12.15 × 15 *Height* 3 ft 3 ins *Weight* 7 cwt *Average speed* 200 plus m.p.h. approx.

The Range Rover combines the strength of the Land-Rover Estate Car with the comfort of the Rover Saloon. With a $3\frac{1}{2}$ litre V8 engine, the vehicle body consists of a steel safety cage to which outside panels, mostly aluminium, are attached. Safety-conscious engineers have placed protective padding where it will do most good in the event of an accident, and there are no hard projections in the car.

ROVER RANGE ROVER SALOON 1971

CHASSIS *Suspension* (*front/rear*) Hydraulic, telescopic shock absorbers

ENGINE *Tank capacity* 19 galls. O.H.V. all-aluminium high performance V8. Bore 3.5 ins (88.9 mm). Stroke 2.8 jns (71.12 mm). Cubic capacity 215 c. ins (3,528 c.c.). 8.5:1 compression ratio. *Max. gross B.H.P.* 156 at 5000 rev/min.

TRANSMISSION *Clutch* Diaphragm spring, single dry plate *Main gearbox* 4 forward, 1 reverse, manually operated with synchromesh on all forward gears *Transfer gearbox* 2 speed reduction type on main gearbox output

STEERING Burman, recirculating ball worm and nut

DIMENSIONS *Length* 176 ins *Width* 70 ins *Wheelbase* 100 ins *Height* 70 ins *Maximum speed* 96 m.p.h.

Winner of Car Of The Year Competition in 1971, the Citroen GS is the four-door saloon launched in 1970 to fill the gap between the Ami 8 and the D. Introduced to Britain in 1971, it marks a milestone in automotive engineering and brings to the small family saloon a degree of sophistication seldom found among the automotive ranks.

CITROEN GS SALOON 1970

CHASSIS Front wheel drive *Brakes* 4 wheel, power operated disc
ENGINE Horizontally opposed 4 cylinder, air-cooled. 1015 c.c. developing 61 b.h.p. at 6750 r.p.m. *Carburettor* Twin choke Solex
TRANSMISSION *Floor* level control *Gearbox* 4 speed synchromesh
STEERING Rack and pinion. Turning circle 30 ft. Specially padded, single spoke, safety steering wheel
DIMENSIONS *Length* 162 ins *Width* 63.30 ins *Wheelbase* 100.40 ins *Height* 53.15 ins *Tyre size* 145/15 *Maximum speed* 91 m.p.h.

TECHNICAL NOTES

One or two terms used in the early days of motoring may not be familiar to present-day readers, as although the basic design of the motor-car has not changed very much over the years, many of the component parts have changes either in design or name.

TUBE IGNITION. In the early days, electricity was regarded with considerable suspicion, and so some manufacturers tried an alternative to the battery and trembler coil that provided the first electric system. This was a tube, closed at the 'outside end', screwed into the cylinder at a convenient position on the side. This tube was then heated to a nice cherry red so that when the piston rose to compress the petrol and air mixture, some of the mixture would be forced into the hot tube where it would ignite. As can be imagined, there were some snags to this system. A strong wind could put out the burner that heated the tube, or an accident could mean spilling some petrol near the burner with spectacular but undesirable results. Another snag was the fact that it was almost impossible to adjust the timing of the ignition, and therefore this type of ignition was only satisfactory on slow-turning engines. A final disadvantage was the cost. The tube had to be platinum, as no other metal would stand the continuous heat.

TREMBLER COIL. The kind of coil fitted to most early cars that had electric ignition was the 'trembler coil'. This was a coil with an inner and an outer winding like a present-day coil. The high voltage required was achieved by switching the current in the outer, or primary coil, by means of the trembler, a small piece of metal with a movement rather like the striker of an electric bell, except that the trembler would switch the current off and on about 10,000 times a minute, thus boosting the current from the secondary coil from about 4 volts to about 10,000 from a coil in good condition and correctly adjusted. Many fifty- or sixty-year-old coils are still giving good service in Veteran cars owned by enthusiasts.

THE MAGNETO. The magneto first became popular about 1904, and after a few years had become the usual method of getting a spark to the plugs of the world's motor-cars. The magneto is a generator driven by the engine, with a built-in contact breaker and distributor. A car's ignition system was therefore contained within a compact little machine. For the first few years the magneto used was the low tension type in which the contact breaker was within each cylinder. This was a very good system and was used by such firms as Mercédès and Italia, but was unnecessarily complicated and more expensive than it need be. So the high tension magneto was evolved, and this was the standard system from about 1906 until the coil was re-introduced around 1930 on the grounds of saving a few pounds on the cost of the car. The magneto was very reliable and it was of course independent of the car's battery. You could run your car happily when the battery was flat. You can't do that with a modern car! The only snag about the magneto is that it does not like dampness very much and the armature needed rewinding about every 5 years.

PRIMING TAPS. As many of the early cars had very big engines (anything below three litres was very definitely a 'mini') swinging the engine to start it when cold could be very hard work indeed. Thus cars had priming taps fitted.

These were little brass taps screwed into the top of each cylinder with a little cup, about half the size of a small teaspoon, into which you poured some petrol. You then opened the taps, let the petrol run into the cylinders, closed the taps again, stuffed a rag into the carburettor air intake, retarding the ignition, set the hand throttle at the position that you had previously found was the best for starting, walked round to the front of the car, and—with a prayer—swung the engine over by means of the starting handle. If you were lucky, the car would start, so you then removed the rag, closed the bonnet and hurriedly got into the driving seat and adjusted the throttle before the vibration shook something off.

THE SPRAG OR DEVIL. This was a long lever fitted to many early cars. The idea was that you let it down so that the end dragged along the road when you were ascending a hill. Then, when and if you missed your gear change (an easy thing to do on some of the early gearboxes, especially as the technique of 'double declutching' was not general much before the First World War), the sprag would dig into the road as soon as the car started to run backwards down the hill. The vital thing was to see that you let it down *before* the car started its backward roll, otherwise the car would leapfrog over the sprag, doing goodness knows what damage. In that event, there was nothing much the driver could do, except either steer and hope for the best, or jump out. Many very early cars had brakes that did not work in reverse!

TYRE SIZES. In the early days, the method of measuring tyre size was different to that used today. In tyres made in Britain and Europe, size was almost always measured in millimetres, while the Americans used inches. The outer circumference was always given first and the thickness of the tyre followed. Thus a tyre described as being 760 x 90 was about 760 mm. in diameter and 90 mm. thick, or wide. (The American equivalent was 30 x $3\frac{1}{2}$). From this you can work out that the wheel itself was 30″ minus $3\frac{1}{2}$″ twice, in other words the wheel was 23″ in diameter. Although many sizes were made, some of them were only manufactured in small numbers. The smaller cars usually fitted 720 x 90 or 760 x 90 tyres, while family cars used the 820 x 120 tyres— roughly equivalent to the 32 x 4 used in America. Some of the early racing cars used very large tyres, a diameter of 40 not being unknown. Anyone finding a car that needed some of these would be in trouble, as they haven't been made for a very long time; but the more usual sizes are still made by Dunlop, especially for racing enthusiasts.

In the early 'twenties, balloon tyres operating at a much lower pressure than the early tyres, were introduced, and at the same time a new system of identification was started. This did not become general for a long time, some manufacturers still using the old system ten years later. Under the new style of identification, the wheel size is given, so that a tyre labelled 4.50 x 19 fitted a wheel 19″ in diameter. If you then added twice the thickness given to the wheel diameter, you arrived at 28″ for the outside diameter of the wheel and tyre combined. This is the system still in use today, and used throughout the world.

The solid tyres that were fitted to the early cars, and to commercial vehicles up until they went over to the pneumatic tyre in the late 'twenties, used much the same system. A typical commercial size was 870 x 110. The size fitted to a

First World War army Dennis was 1060 x 130 x 88, the second number, being the width of the tyre, and the third number the thickness of the tyre. New tyres made for such vehicles are labelled with the more recent style.

COACHWORK. In the early days of motoring, the enthusiast bought his car from the makers, or their agents, and in most cases what he got was the bare chassis. The idea of having standard bodywork fitted to a car did not appeal to the relatively well-off buyers of the time. The customer ordered his car, and when ready it was delivered straight to the coachbuilder, there being at least one coachbuilder in any town of note. The style and design of the body to be built being decided, the coachbuilder then went ahead, and this tended to be a lengthy business. The whole operation would probably take three months to carry out, at least three weeks of this time being devoted to the painting alone. Because of this, the size of many early cars rather depended on the coachwork fitted, so sizes quoted may not necessarily be correct for the car of the same model fitted with a different type of body. Even the mudguards can alter the width by several inches, although they did tend to become standard fittings.

This state of affairs persisted well into the 'twenties with the large cars, although most of the popular cars had standard bodywork after the First World War. But even with popular cars, there was often a wide range of styles to choose from, and it was not unusual to have two length of chassis for the same car—one for the family type and the other a shorter sports model.

In the late 'twenties, bumpers became popular, and these could be fitted to a car at the owner's request, but on many makes they did not become standard until well into the 'thirties. Some cars only got bumpers as standard fittings just before the Second World War.

By the Second World War, the 'coach built' body—a body built by making a wooden frame and then covering the frame with panels of metal—was fast disappearing in favour of the all-metal pressed steel body, with all its snags, that we know today. The modern method of painting with cellulose or synthetic paint sprayed first became popular in the late 'twenties; before then, all the paint had been applied by hand with a paint brush.

It was usual for the fittings on a car made before the First World War to be finished as polished brass, although nickel plate was used for several years before the war on some makes. After the war, nickel plate became the usual finish for all the metal fittings, and this also required much work with metal polish to keep it looking smart. In the 'twenties, the radiator was usually made of 'German silver', an alloy of copper, zinc and nickel, which polished up very nicely with a bit of effort, but soon looked dull when it rained.

In 1928, chromium plating was introduced in America, and, because it did away with the hard task of polishing the metal work, immediately became very popular. Within a year or so, almost all cars on the market were being fitted with chromium-plated parts instead of the softer, warmer nickel.

In the 'twenties and 'thirties mudguards were almost always painted black, because this colour is so much easier to match in the event of a minor scrape than any other colour. A few minutes' work with a hammer and a tin of black paint was sufficient to restore smartness to a car after quite a nasty bump—much easier than it is today with the thin pressed steel bodies and the hard-to-match colours that always seem to show the slightest scratch.

	Page		Page		Page
Abarth 1968	155	Chrysler 1963	142	Fiat 1967	154
Adler 1910	49	Citroen 1934	95	Ford 1908	43
Adler 1914	59	Citroen 1955	126	Ford 1923	75
Alfa-Romeo 1924	77	Citroen 1956	129	Ford 1933	94
Alvis 1924	78	Clyno 1923	74	Ford 1966	151
Austin 1922	72	Crossley 1913	53	Frazer Nash 1934	97
Austin 1923	73	Crossley 1929	85	G.N. 1919	63
Austin 1930	87	Cugnot's Steam Tractor		Hillman 1963	143
Austin 1936	100	1770	4	Hispano-Suiza 1928	83
Austin 1952	121	DAF 1958	133	Humber 1953	123
Austin 1959–61	136	Daimler 1897	21	Hupmobile 1909	45
Auto Union 1936	93	Daimler 1906	37	International Harvester	
Bean 1920	65	Daimler 1928	82	1907	40
Bentley 1929	86	Daimler 1953	124	Itala 1907	41
BMC Mini 1959	135	Darracq 1904	31	Jaguar 1948	116
B.M.W. 1936	101	De Dion Bouton 1903	30	Jaguar 1961	138
Bond 1964	145	Delage 1929	84	Jaguar 1968	2
Bristol 1947	112	Delaunay-Belleville 1914	61	Jensen 1966	152
Bugatti 1914	58	Ferrari 1965	146	Jowett 1910	48
Buick 1905	35	Ferrari 1967	153	Lagonda 1913	55
Cadillac 1903	29	Fiat 1901	24	Lanchester 1897	20
Catley and Ayes Steam		Fiat 1905	34	Lancia 1922	70
Wagonette 1868	17	Fiat 1912–1915	51	Lancia 1952	122
Chevrolet 1914	60	Fiat 1919	62	Maserati 1957	131
Chevrolet 1935	98	Fiat 1922	69	Maybach 1938	107
Chevrolet 1966	150	Fiat 1932	92	Mercedes 1902	26
Chrysler 1934	96	Fiat 1936–48	102	Mercer 1921	68

	Page		Page		Page
M.G. 1932	91	Renault 1931	90	Vauxhall 1913	56
M.G. 1950	120	Renault 1947	113	Vauxhall 1936	104
M.M.C. 1897	22	Renault 1956	130	Vauxhall 1955	127
Morgan 1920	66	Riley 1926	81	Volkswagen 1936	105
Morris 1919	64	Riley 1946–53	110	Volkswagen 1960	137
Morris 1930	89	Riley 1962	141	Volkswagen 1965	149
Morris 1937	106	Roger Benz 1888	18	Volvo 1955	128
Morris 1939	108	Rolls Royce 1904	32	Wolseley 1902–3	27
Morris 1948	117	Rolls Royce 1906	39	Wolseley 1930	88
Morris 1949	119	Rolls Royce 1936	103	Wolseley 1939	109
Morris 1961–64	144	Rolls Royce 1947	115		
Mors 1903	28	Rolls Royce 1965	147		
Napier 1913	57	Rover 1904	33		
NSU 1958	132	Rover 1954	125		
Oldsmobile 1900	23	Rover–B.R.M. 1965	148		
Oldsmobile 1910	50	Russo-Baltique 1909	47		
O.M. 1924	79	Singer 1959	134		
Opel 1908	44	S.S. (Jaguar) 1935	99		
Panhard 1901	25	Standard 1906	38		
Panhard Levassor 1894	19	Standard 1947	114		
Peugeot 1912	52	Stanley 1907	42		
Peugeot 1913	54	Storey 1920	67		
Peugeot 1948	118	Swift 1909	46		
Pontiac 1961	139	Swift 1924	80		
Porsche 1962	140	Triumph 1946	111		
Renault 1906	37	Trojan 1922	71		
Renault 1923	76	Vauxhall 1905	12		